LEAVING GLORYTOWN

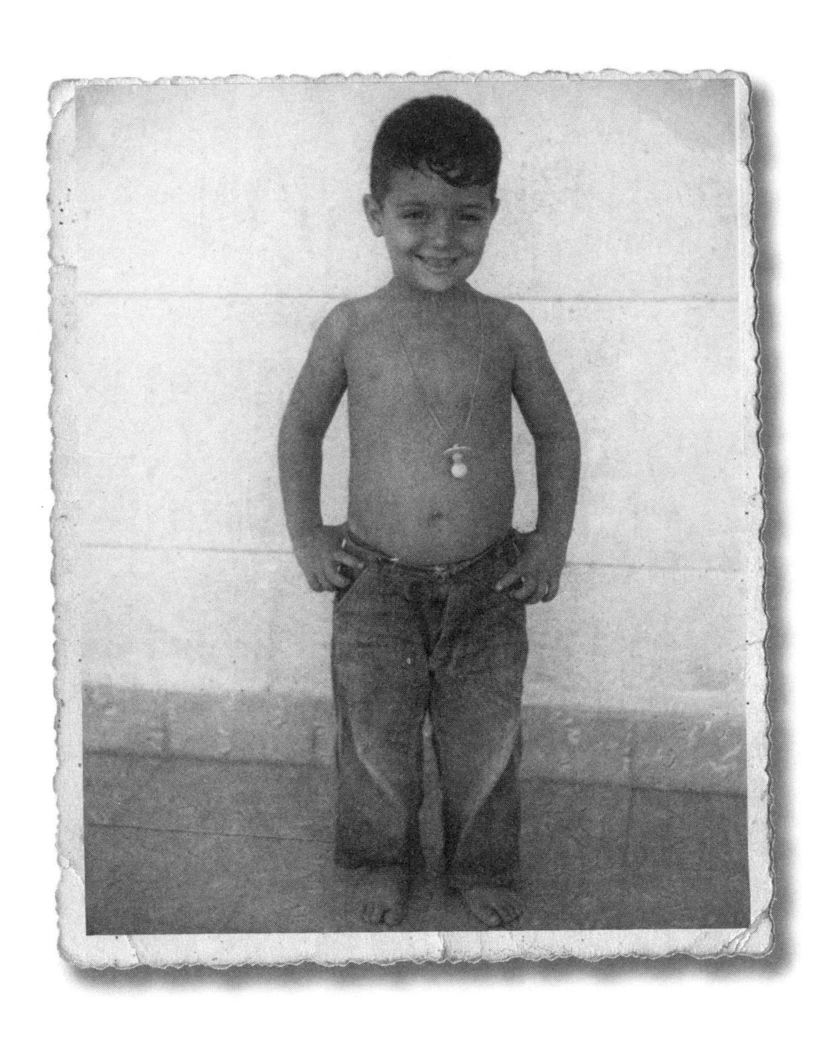

LEAVING GLORYTOWN

One Boy's Struggle Under Castro

Eduardo F. Calcines

Farrar Straus Giroux • New York

Distributed in Canada by Douglas & McIntyre Ltd.
Printed in the United States of America
Designed by Irene Metaxatos
First edition, 2009
10 9 8 7 6 5 4 3 2 1

www.fsgkidsbooks.com

Library of Congress Cataloging-in-Publication Data
Calcines, Eduardo F.
Leaving Glorytown : one boy's struggle under Castro / Eduardo F. Calcines.— 1st ed.
p. cm.
ISBN-13: 978-0-374-34394-1
ISBN-10: 0-374-34394-2
1. Calcines, Eduardo F. 2. Cuba—History—1959–1990. 3. Cubans—Biography.
4. Refugees—United States—Biography. I. Title.

CT518.C35C35 2009
972.9106'4092—dc22
[B]

2008007506

In loving memory of
my father, Rafael, of Tío William,
and of my grandparents,
Ana and Julian

Contents

Introduction

I was a child of Communism. This means I was raised in two worlds—one a world of ideals, the other the real world. The world of ideals was full of Fidel Castro's lying propaganda and empty promises of a better tomorrow. The real world was even worse: a world of oppression, hunger, fear, poverty, and violence.

To an outsider visiting Cuba, there would have been nothing special about my family. We were not rich, famous, or politically well-connected. We suffered neither more nor less than any other family of dissidents who were frantic to get out of what had become a living nightmare. What made us remarkable is that we survived and escaped.

Everything in this book is true in its depiction of Cuban life. Although I have now lived in the United States for forty years, I decided that it is time to let the world know not only what happened to my family, but also what happened—and continues to happen today—to all the people of Cuba, from whom Fidel Castro has taken everything, including hope itself.

Esther and Eduardo Calcines

Felo and Conchita Calcines

Tío William

Abuela and Abuelo Espinosa

LEAVING GLORYTOWN

Coming to Glorytown

God made everything and everyone. He even made Fidel Castro. That's what my *abuelos*, or grandparents, Ana and Julian Espinosa, always taught me. That meant the Revolution was God's doing, too. At the very least, He allowed it to happen.

When I was a boy, that made no sense to me. I wanted to know if we were being punished or tested. Nobody could tell me for sure. Abuela Ana wasn't complaining—she never complained about anything. She merely observed that God didn't miss a beat. We Cubans might have felt that He had abandoned us, but that wasn't true.

No.

It was the rest of the world that had forgotten about the people of Cuba.

That's what Abuela Ana said. And she should know, because even before Castro came to power when he overthrew the dictatorship of Fulgencio Batista, life had been hard for my family.

☆

Maybe Cuba's problems—and ours—started with sugarcane. Sugar is the lifeblood of Cuba, and the central province of Las Villas, where my people came from, is the heart of sugarcane country.

But farming sugarcane is brutally hard work. Both of my grandfathers had begun toiling under the Caribbean sun before they hit puberty: hacking at the tough canes with machetes, slapping insects, watching out for snakes, and hoping their exhausted neighbor's aim didn't go awry. In the old days, this was slave work. Each of my grandfathers dreamed of leaving as soon as he could, in search of a better life. Only my maternal grandfather, Abuelo Julian, managed to do that when he put down his machete and left the cane fields in the farming town of Rodas in Las Villas in 1918.

My other abuelo, Alfonso Calcines, was a sharecropper in the town of Cumanayagua. He and my abuela Petra had seventeen children, twelve of whom survived childhood. My father, Rafael, whom everyone called Felo, was their youngest son. They rented a small house on land owned by a wealthy Spaniard. In return for their labor, they were allowed to keep part of the sugar crop. This provided them with their basic needs for food, clothing, and shelter—but nothing else.

When my father was eight, one of his brothers was killed in a shooting accident, and my grandfather died suddenly of "grief"—probably either a heart attack or an aneurysm. He left his family nothing but the clothes on his back and a few pieces of furniture. The wealthy Spaniard had no use for the rest of the family, so he told them to get off his land and make sure they didn't take anything that didn't belong to them. Even the machete was his.

Abuela Petra had a brother in the city of Cienfuegos. He offered to take in the family until they could get back on their feet. So one day

Abuela Petra and her remaining children—in addition to the one who was shot, four others had died of childhood maladies—walked thirty miles along the dusty roads of rural Cuba until they arrived at their new home.

Cienfuegos was called Cacicazgo de Jagua in the eighteenth century, when it was founded, then Fernandina de Jagua in the nineteenth century, and finally, Cienfuegos, after a Spanish *capitán general*. But its nickname has always been La Perla del Sur, the Pearl of the South. The buildings are well-constructed and elegant. Cienfuegos boasts the most geometrically perfect street plan in Cuba, perhaps in all of the Caribbean. It's said that one can shoot an arrow through the heart of town without ever striking a building. Before Castro came to power, the port bustled with ships sailing under every kind of flag. A majestic Spanish fort, El Castillo de Jagua, still dominates the turquoise waters of the bay.

Some members of both the Calcines and Espinosa tribes eventually ended up in the *barrio*, or neighborhood, of Glorytown. My parents met when my mother was fourteen, my father twenty-one. One of my mother's sisters, Violeta, was my father's neighbor. It was during one of my mother's frequent visits to see her sister that my father noticed her and began to think about settling down.

Felo had already been laboring for years on the docks, where he and his brothers had earned reputations as tireless workers. Decent-paying jobs for uneducated, untrained men were scarce, and they got used to defending their positions with the only means of arbitration they had—their fists. But if another laborer collapsed under the brutal sun, as was common, one of the Calcines brothers would be there to carry the fallen man's load as well as his own. This way, although dockhands were paid by the load, the fallen man would receive his full pay at the end of the day.

My mother, Conchita, was flattered by Felo's attention. For three years, they invented reasons to bump into each other accidentally-on-purpose on the sidewalk outside Violeta's home. It was improper for them to talk privately before being formally introduced, and that couldn't happen until Conchita was a little older. But the sidewalk was public territory, and their families could keep an eye on them, so the normal restrictions governing courtship were relaxed. In 1953, they were married on June 19—the same day my abuelos Ana and Julian Espinosa had gotten married in 1911.

My mother had been a sickly child, and when she became pregnant with me, Abuela Ana was worried. But she needn't have been. My mother was tough, as the youngest of eleven must be, and Abuela herself would be there to handle whatever came up.

Childbirth was one of Abuela's numerous specialties. She'd assisted at the births of all her twenty-nine grandchildren so far. But number thirty, she would say later, was the most difficult, because I wanted nothing to do with this world. I simply refused to leave the womb. As a precaution, Conchita had gone to a birthing clinic, along with Abuela Ana and Papa, but somehow no one noticed until it was nearly too late that the clinic had no forceps. My father ran out and borrowed a pair, and it turned out to be too small. But it had to do.

The doctor dug deep, searching for my head, and in the process he nearly tore apart my left eye. Eventually, after a long struggle, I was born on October 4, 1955.

Abuela Ana and Abuelo Julian had just bought a house at 6110 San

Carlos Street—the first they ever owned. My parents lived in a room that Abuelo had added on to the back in anticipation of my birth. It had a bed, a cabinet, a small bathroom, and a window that looked out on the backyard.

The yard was small, maybe twenty by thirty-five feet, but it was filled with mature tropical fruit trees: coconut, avocado, lemon, grapefruit, orange, and the applelike *nispero*, or loquat. Their thick branches and broad leaves formed a canopy that cast a cool shade over the entire yard. This made it the perfect place to raise a few chickens, as well as their rooster, Pichilingo, who would become my best friend. In later years, I would spend hours sitting on the tile roof, learning how to communicate with tropical songbirds in their own language and envying them their ability to fly away.

The injury to my eye was painful. I had surgery at the age of one, and again at two. These operations were ultimately successful, but I had a lot of sleepless nights, according to Mama. She often said that her only company in those wee hours was Pichilingo, who scratched and crowed anxiously as I cried out my agony to the night sky.

I was a lucky kid, in the best way a kid can be lucky: I was loved. It was really as if I had four doting parents—my own, and Abuela Ana and Abuelo Julian. Of course, Abuela Petra loved me, too, but since she lived far away in another barrio, I saw her only occasionally and then she died in 1962, when I was six. It was Ana and Julian who looked after me constantly while Papa worked and Mama was busy doing chores around the house. I even took my first steps clutching my grandparents' fingers. They eventually had more than one hundred grandchildren and great-grandchildren, but I was always the closest.

Abuela Ana was only four feet tall, but she was energetic and powerful, and when she wanted to, she could make herself appear to double in height. She was afraid of nothing and no one.

People in my family loved to tell the story of Abuela and the Mysterious Fingers. One night, when Abuelo was away, Abuela heard a noise coming from the doors to her house, as if they were being pushed or scratched on. At first she thought it was a mouse. But the noise was more sinister than that. Sensing danger, Abuela went for her machete, which in Cuba is a common household implement. Abuela used hers for cutting the heads off chickens, so she kept it nice and sharp.

As she approached the doors, she noticed a hand reaching in from underneath, trying to loosen the lock on the floor. She swung the blade and hit the concrete floor near the intruder's hand, meanwhile screaming at the top of her lungs, "I recognize your fingers, mister, and I know who you are! The next time you try to unlock my doors, I won't miss!"

Abuela had no idea whose fingers they were. But the man disappeared faster than a snake slides through the grass, for he had just tasted the wrath of Ana Espinosa, and he was not about to stick around for a second helping. By the next day, the story had spread around the whole barrio. It was a testament to Abuela Ana's character that she didn't actually cut the man's fingers off.

"Maybe he had children to feed," Abuela said, retelling this story to me and my little *hermana*, or sister, Esther, years later. "Maybe he felt such shame at being poor that he had no choice but to steal. Why should he lose his fingers over that? Look at us now. We've lost everything, and it's not even our fault. We're probably in the same state as that poor man was then. How glad I am that I showed him mercy and let him keep his fingers! Otherwise, who knows how much worse God would be punishing me now?"

Mama and Papa soon moved out of the back room and rented a house across the street, but Ana and Julian's backyard remained my favorite place. I was their *niño*, their boy, and I could do whatever I wanted—within reason. If I did something wrong at home, all I had to do was run across the street. Mama would chase me right up to the front porch of Abuela Ana's house. She would yell, throw things, and threaten to tell Papa, but that was as far as she could go. Abuela would hear the commotion and race out front, her kitchen apron slung over her shoulder. She would grab me and press my head into her large, soft chest.

"Now, Conchita," she would say, "go take care of your home, and let me take care of your *hijo*, your son. Poor thing, look how scared he is!"

"Spoiled, that's what he is," Mama would say. "And it's your fault, Mama! You let him get away with murder, because you're his grandmother!"

"Oh, go on. It's a grandmother's job to spoil her grandkids," Abuela would reply, still pressing my face into her bosom.

Abuela had nursed eleven children. I thought she probably had the largest breasts in the world. They reached all the way to her waist, which was just the right height for suffocating a small child like me. Sometimes I didn't know which was worse: Mama's wrath or Abuela's embrace. To avoid them both, I learned at an early age to climb the avocado tree in Abuela and Abuelo's backyard and get onto their roof. That became my means of escaping all the dangers of the world.

Every May, our family eagerly awaited Abuelo Julian's return from his three- or four-month sojourn at the sugar mill, where he supervised the cane harvest and enjoyed the grand title of First Sugar Master. He had come a long way from his days as a simple field hand in Rodas. My heart would pound in anticipation of the festivities that always came with this blessed event. My wealthy and generous *tío*, or uncle, William would buy a pig that weighed three or four times as much as I did. The men would cut its throat, gut it, and shave the long, bristly hairs from its skin with their razor-sharp machetes. Then they would dig a deep pit, build a massive fire, and lower the pig on a tray close to the coals. Several hours later, it would be roasted to perfection, and we would all stuff ourselves. As often as not, such a feast would turn into an impromptu block party, with all the neighbors showing up bearing special dishes and bottles of rum. Then the celebration would go on all night.

I looked forward to Abuelo Julian's return more than anyone, because when he was home, we were inseparable. From the time I was old enough to cross the street on my own, I sat patiently in the backyard every morning with Pichilingo, waiting for Abuela Ana to get up and open the back doors. She would give me a kiss and toss some breadcrumbs on the ground for the chickens. Then she'd usher me in and hand me a cup of coffee to take to Abuelo in bed. He'd sit up, ignoring Abuela's jibes about how long it took him to wake up these days, and drink it down in one gulp. Next he'd shave, put on some delicious-smelling aftershave, and comb his hair with scented water.

I watched all this in fascination. One of the first lessons I learned in life was that even a man of modest means should take pride in his appearance—not out of arrogance, but to show the rest of the world that he respects himself, and therefore is worthy of respect.

Once Abuelo Julian was up, the day was ours. My favorite thing to do with him was to play catch as we listened to baseball games from Havana on the radio.

"Niño, you're going to be a star someday!" he said. "But not if you throw like that! Come on, throw hard!"

"Julian," Abuela said from the back of the house, "aren't you a little too old to be playing ball? All we need is for you to break your glasses—or your leg!"

Abuelo smiled and whispered, "Throw it as hard as you can. Don't worry about Abuela. She worries too much, anyway."

Then, in a louder voice, he said, "Yes, my love. I know. But don't you worry. I'm not as old as you think!"

The Revolution

One morning in January 1959, I woke up and noticed immediately, in my childlike way, that something was wrong. I crawled out of bed and found Mama and Papa listening to the radio. They were so rapt that they ignored me. If I'd peed on the floor, they wouldn't have noticed. A Voice on the radio droned on and on. Mama even forgot to give me breakfast. This was not right. I was used to being the center of attention at all times, and I wasn't going to give up my place without a fight.

Yet it didn't seem to matter what I did. My parents and abuelos were so distracted by the Voice that even my tantrums didn't work.

In the next weeks, I noticed soldiers on every corner. This, I thought, was a great thing. I was fascinated by the way the sun gleamed on the soldiers' olive helmets and sleek, black weapons. I loved to watch the military jeeps careen around town, filled with self-important officers in their black-visored caps.

Loudspeakers went up on light poles all over town and began to broadcast the Voice. There were loudspeakers on cars, too, also playing recorded speeches by the Voice, over and over, each one vying to be the loudest. They were out of sync with one another, so that the air became a crazy tapestry of the same Voice at different intervals, volumes, and pitches. Who was this Voice? I had no idea, but I figured he was someone important. I was only three years old and so much of the world was a mystery to me—it was just one more thing to be puzzled over.

One day, Abuela Ana and I were walking to the store to get some milk when I heard a tremendous roar. We found a spot on the sidewalk among a rapidly growing crowd. The roar grew closer. At the last moment, I lost my nerve and dived behind Abuela's skirt. Peeking out, I beheld an amazing sight: hundreds and hundreds of people, marching, chanting, and singing. The pounding of their feet resounded in my chest. They yelled, *Viva Fidel!* and *Viva la Revolución!* Long live Fidel! Long live the Revolution! I still had no idea what a revolution was. So far, it was all army men and marches, and both of those things were fine with me.

The Voice could talk for hours. I could leave the radio to take a nap, wake up two or three hours later, and he would still be talking. At first I was impressed, then bored. Soon the Voice faded into the background of my life. It seemed that it had always been there, like our house, like my parents and grandparents, like Pichilingo. I paid no more attention to it than to the color of the walls.

The next thing I noticed was that the grownups of my world seemed unhappy. They snapped at me for little things, and they acted as if something was wrong. I assumed it was because I was a bad boy, so I did my best to stop tracking dirt in the house and to listen when told to pick up my toys. But that made no difference. Everyone stayed upset, no matter what I did.

We had less to eat now. Our favorite meals had been beans or rice, served with all kinds of meat—pork, chicken, or beef—and seasoned with hot peppers or fresh herbs. We'd never been wealthy, but we'd always had enough food. Now, at dinnertime, there was less on my plate. I'd always loved ketchup, but now there was none to be found. We could still get rice and beans, and there were fruit trees in Abuela Ana and Abuelo Julian's yard, but I often couldn't eat as much as I wanted. I thought I was being punished for something, and I cried out of frustration—hadn't I been doing my best to behave well?

"Don't cry, niño," Papa told me. "There's no point. And besides, men don't cry. They fight back against the things they can change, and they don't complain about the things they cannot."

"He's not even four!" Mama said. "Don't talk to him about fighting."

"It's not too early for him to start learning how the world works," Papa said. "It's the world he has to live in, after all."

"Tell him he's a good boy," said Mama. "He thinks you're mad at him for something."

"You *are* a good boy, hijo," said Papa, mussing my hair. "It's the world that's going bad."

I was relieved to hear that my efforts at self-improvement had not gone unnoticed. But things didn't get any better.

My father rose every morning well before the sun. I was very proud of Papa. After he had married Mama, he had left the docks and become a driver. Anyone who was even vaguely associated with engines was important in my eyes, but to be a driver was the greatest thing of all.

Papa was a driver for Tío William, who owned a distribution company, and my wild and crazy Tío Cholu, Mama's middle brother, was his assistant. Tío William was Mama's oldest brother, and he was a big man in every sense. Because of his success in life, he was treated with reverence, and on top of that he weighed nearly three hundred pounds. Like many other members of Mama's family, he, too, lived on San Carlos Street. He had two sons, Julian and Gilberto, and a daughter, Carmensita, whom I often played with when I wasn't hanging out with my friends, Rolando and Tito Caballero, and my cousin Luis. Carmensita was five years older than I was, but she treated me as an equal, and I loved it.

I learned that in this strange new world of the Revolution, Tuesday was the day to look forward to. That was when Papa and Tío Cholu went out to the countryside to deliver gasoline and alcohol to the farmers. They would come back from these trips after dark, bearing wonderful things: pieces of fresh beef, a dozen eggs, soft loaves of bread, a whole chicken. Then we would eat the way we used to.

Once night after supper, Papa said, "Niño, go play. I need to talk to your mama."

I obeyed, but I stayed within earshot. I could make out Papa's low tones: ". . . got to get out of here . . . ," ". . . leave the country for America . . . ," ". . . exit visa."

I burst back into the kitchen, which doubled as our dining room.

"Are we going on a trip?" I yelled. But I was unprepared for Papa's anger.

"Quiet!" he thundered. He went to the front door, opened it, and looked up and down the sidewalk. Then he came back to where I stood.

Tears were rolling down my face. Papa was a gentle, affectionate man who hardly ever raised his voice, and when he did, it was shocking. He grabbed me by the shoulders, but then he looked at me tenderly.

"Do you see," he said to Mama. "Here I am, yelling at my son because I'm afraid the government will hear what he thinks. Is this any way for us to live? Do we need any more reason to get out of here?"

"Felo, be careful what you say in front of him," Mama murmured. "He could repeat it."

"Eduar," Papa said, "I love you more than anything, and I'm sorry I yelled at you. But there is something you must understand. If the bad people hear what we're talking about, we could all get in big trouble. So don't ever again say anything about us leaving—nothing is decided anyway. Understand?"

Miserable, I nodded.

"Buck up," he said. "Real men don't cry just because of a little yelling."

"Yes, Papa."

"You know I love you, niño. Give me a hug."

I didn't need to be told twice to hug Papa. He smelled of aftershave, like Abuelo Julian, and his warm body vibrated when he talked and laughed. I could have clung to him all day like a baby monkey, just to be close to him. But already I knew that it was unmanly to want too much affection. A man had to be tough, and I was going to be a man—a big, strong one, just like Papa.

After that, there were a lot of late-night conversations between my parents and grandparents. I overheard them from my bed near the porch, though I understood little of what was being said. I knew only that Mama would sometimes cry—normally a rare occurrence—and that everyone else sounded worried.

Sometimes Tío William would sit in on these conversations, too. Tío William was a hero to us all, and his opinion carried great weight—just like he did. His voice echoed through the night like the call of a bull elephant. You could feel it as much as hear it. Everyone listened to Tío William. I never paid attention to his actual words, though—I was too busy thrilling to his deep tones, which I could feel through the springs of my bed.

Because I played with Carmensita, I saw a lot of Tío William. But one morning, when I walked into their house—none of us ever bothered knocking—she was nowhere to be found.

"Tía!" I said to my aunt Carmen. "Where is Carmensita?"

"Shh!" said Tía Carmen. "Carmensita is in bed. She doesn't feel good."

"What's wrong with her?"

"She has a fever," said Tía Carmen. "You go away and come back tomorrow, Eduar. She'll be better by then. The doctor says she has the flu."

But the next day, Carmensita was worse. Now, in addition to her fever, she had aches and pains.

"Carmensita!" I yelled from the living room. "Come out and play!"

Carmensita poked her head around the corner of her parents' bedroom.

"Okay!" she said weakly.

But her mother pushed her back into bed. Then she came out and led me to the door.

"Eduar," she said, "you must leave at once. It's not safe for you to be here. You might catch what she has."

"I want Carmensita!" I wailed.

"Just go!" said Tía Carmen. "We'll tell you when it's safe to come back."

By late afternoon their house was full of grownups, but I still wasn't allowed inside. Then the men carried Carmensita out of the house on a stretcher and into a waiting car. I was in their front yard and I called her name as she went by, but she didn't respond. She was asleep. She looked very pretty and peaceful, I thought, though I was surprised that she could sleep through all the fun of going for a stretcher ride.

It was the last time I ever saw her. They took her to a hospital in Havana, but it was too late. The next day, I was told that Carmensita had gone to heaven, and that I would not see her again in this lifetime.

I could hear my father cursing in the kitchen. This time, he didn't care who heard him.

"That damn useless doctor!" he shouted. "If all the good doctors hadn't left the country because of this stupid Revolution, they would have found out what was wrong with her!"

But my father's reaction was nothing compared to Tío William's. He shut himself up in his house and refused to come out for days. The whole neighborhood could hear his screams of rage and heartbreak. *Why? Why, God? Why did you take my baby girl from me? What did I do to deserve this?* No one, not his sons, Julian and Gilberto, not even Tía Carmen, could go near him.

The Bay of Pigs

In the spring of 1961, when I was five and a half, I heard a great commotion on the street from my rooftop perch under the fruit trees: truck and jeep engines, strange men shouting orders, women screaming, children crying. I didn't know whether to stay in hiding or go look. Finally I climbed down and went timidly to my grandparents' front door.

There, in our ordinarily tranquil street, I beheld chaos. Soldiers with weapons were everywhere. Their eyes were as flat and glittering as a snake's, and their faces were full of menace. Worse, they were pointing their guns at people. I'd never seen them do that before. All the men in the neighborhood knelt in a row, hands on their heads, looking down at the ground. Some of the soldiers were holding their guns to the men's heads, and it seemed that they might shoot at any moment.

Then, to my horror, I saw that Papa and Tío William were among the kneeling men. The soldiers snarled at everyone to keep still and do as they were told. Meanwhile, an officer was strutting back and forth, screaming in a high-pitched voice at the women to stop their crying and let the soldiers do their job, or they would all be arrested, too.

Rooted where I stood, I saw my mother approach this officer, wringing her apron in her hands. She asked him something. His response was to lift his hand as if to hit her. My mother stood her ground, unflinching. She repeated her question several more times, and finally the officer gave her some kind of curt answer.

Then they loaded the men—including Papa and Tío William—into the trucks and drove off. Standing at the door, I tried to yell Papa's name, but I could make only a hoarse sound. I could see his face as they drove off. I had never seen him look frightened before.

When the trucks were gone, Mama yelled, "They're taking them to the Terry Theater!"

A wail went up from the women. I didn't understand—were the men being taken to a puppet show? Somehow I didn't think so, but I could imagine no other reason for going to the theater.

At last I dared to venture out of the house. When Mama saw me, she grabbed me and held me tight.

"What's happening?" I asked.

"Nothing, niño," she said. "Don't worry. Everything will be fine."

By then I'd learned that whenever someone said everything was going to be fine, things were about to get really bad. And I was right. We spent a long, tense night huddled up together—me, Mama, and my baby sister, Esther, who was only six months old. Esther slept, and eventually so did I. I'm sure Mama didn't close her eyes for a moment.

The next day Mama refused to let me out of her sight, and when I said I would go out anyway, she threatened to tie me to a table leg. At first I was defiant, but then came a new sound, the most terrifying yet: Castro's warplanes. They screamed and dived overhead, scaring little Esther so badly that she wouldn't nurse. Trucks full of soldiers zoomed past again, but they didn't stop this time. Something big was going on.

During a lull in the action, Mama ran from house to house with Esther in her arms, knocking on doors. I followed.

"Come to our house," she told everyone. "It's the smallest on the block! If the bombs start falling, it will be the least likely to get hit!"

Many of the residents of San Carlos Street followed us home. There were about twenty-five of us, and those who had chickens or goats brought them along, and the animals ran all over the house. It was like a big party. Babies cried, goats bleated, chickens cackled, and grownups tried to listen over the din to what was happening outside. People ventured out from time to time, but for the most part we stayed inside. Every time a plane went overhead we all squeezed into our large bathroom—it was about ten by fourteen feet. I thought it was very funny that so many of us were in there together.

Finally Mama told me what was happening: the Bay of Pigs was being invaded by the Yankees. Papa and all the other men had been taken away and locked in the Terry Theater so they couldn't join the invaders and fight against the Communists. I knew there wasn't a person on earth who could hurt Papa, who was strong, smart, and capable. I trusted that he would be all right. Since I was an animal lover, my concern was for the pigs. I was worried they might get shot.

Mama laughed, for the first time since Papa had been taken. "There are no real pigs in the Bay of Pigs," she said.

"There must be!" I insisted. "They swim around with their snouts in the air!"

"No, niño, listen. The Bay of Pigs gets its name from a kind of fish that lives there."

I was crestfallen. I'd never heard of the Bay of Pigs before that day, but it sounded like my kind of place. I wanted to believe that it was a porcine paradise, with lots of pink piglets floating on their backs, kicking their legs as they sunned their fat little tummies. I would have loved to visit such a beach.

"Are you sure, Mama?" I asked.

"Yes, niño. When you pull a triggerfish out of the water, it makes a sound like a pig's. Listen: *roik, roik!*"

"Mama," I said, as everyone laughed at her joke, "you're being silly. There is no fish that sounds like a pig. Only pigs sound like pigs. Fish don't make any noise!"

"Okay, niño," Mama said. "You're right. Maybe after this is all over, Papa will take us on a vacation there, and you can see for yourself what it is all about."

Soon the planes and trucks stopped, and the neighbors left. For a long time, I referred to the Bay of Pigs invasion as "the day we all went to the bathroom together."

Three days later, Papa came home, hungry, dehydrated, and stinking to high heaven.

"Give me some water," he said to Mama, collapsing in a chair.

But she wouldn't let him rest until he got into the bathtub. She left the door open, and he told her what had happened to them at the Terry Theater as he scrubbed himself.

"They packed us in there like chickens in a crate," he said. "They nailed the doors and windows shut, and there wasn't a breath of air. If you had to—well, you know—you had to do it right where you stood, in your pants. No food. Hardly any water. A lot of men collapsed. I wouldn't be surprised if some of them died. Concha, I could eat a whole pig right now and it would barely fill the hole in me!"

"They didn't take Rolando and Tito Caballero's father!" I said.

"That's because Caballero is a Communist!" Papa said. "They rounded us up because they didn't want us to fight back! They don't want us being unfaithful, so they treat us like animals. There is no more certain way to turn men against you than to take them away from their families. Concha, we are going to find a way to America, do you hear me?"

"I do, and so does the C.D.R. lady," said Mama. "So keep your voice down."

I was old enough now to understand what C.D.R. meant—the Committee for the Defense of the Revolution. The C.D.R. was kind of a cross between the Gestapo and a Neighbor Watch program. Every residential block in Cuba had a C.D.R. agent living on it—a regular neighbor who had been selected for his or her revolutionary zeal and willingness to inform on neighbors. The agent was often a woman, because in those days women stayed home all day, and they saw everything that happened on the street. It was the C.D.R. agent's job to report any antirevolutionary talk or behavior. Agents marched into people's homes unannounced whenever the Voice was talking, just to make sure they were listening to the radio. These people also kept an eye out for signs of illegal capitalist activity—that is, buying and selling of anything, even food or clothing, on the black market—and listened in on private conversations from doorways and windowsills, hoping to overhear someone making a comment that could get him or her thrown into prison. People who were judged antirevolutionary needed to be re-educated. Re-education was achieved in one of three ways: forced labor, imprisonment, or firing squad.

Sadly, even some of our family members were getting caught up in the madness, including my cousin Peruchito, the son of Abuela Ana's oldest daughter, Idalia. Peruchito actually joined the military.

Mama would tell us the story of the time Peruchito came to visit Abuela Ana and Abuelo Julian in full military dress. As he walked through the front door, he noticed that the framed photograph of Fidel he'd sent was nowhere to be found. "Abuela!" he said. "Where is the photo of El Comandante? You should take down this picture of Jesus and replace it with Fidel. He is the only one who can save us, not some long-haired Jew!"

Abuela threw her apron over her shoulder—always a sign that she was preparing for action—and jabbed Peruchito in the chest with one iron-strong finger.

"Look, young man," she said. "The photo of your so-called leader is in the back room, facedown, with a glass of water over it. And our Jesus will remain on the wall as long as I live."

Placing a photograph facedown meant "rest in peace," in this case expressing a wish that Fidel would die. It was about as antirevolutionary a statement as one could make. And the glass of water with no flowers in it meant that no one would miss Fidel if he died. Peruchito turned and walked out of the house, never to return. We wondered if he would report his own grandmother, but nothing ever came of the incident.

Peruchito died in an automobile accident in which all four passengers were burned beyond recognition. This was a common way for Fidel to do in his enemies—kill them, then make it look as if they'd died in a traffic accident. Peruchito must have fallen afoul of El Comandante somehow.

"Funny how cars have suddenly developed a tendency to burst into flame all the time," Mama said wryly. "I don't remember that happening before the Revolution."

"And it just goes to show you," added Papa, "that you're no better off supporting Castro. Whether you're with him or against him, chances are you're going to end up dead. Better to get as far away from him as possible—as soon as possible!"

Our Last Noche Buena

On December 24, 1961, our entire extended family—nearly two hundred people—and our neighbors gathered on San Carlos Street to celebrate Noche Buena, or Holy Night. This was an annual event, and the highlight of the year. I was happiest when surrounded by my family, and Noche Buena was the one night when we all came together, to celebrate our connection to each other and to rejoice in the birth of Baby Jesus.

The Noche Buena gathering was also a time to tell stories of previous celebrations that had gone hilariously awry. I listened as Papa told the tale of a pig that Tío William had bought, which had escaped before it could be slaughtered. Every fleet-footed man and boy in Glorytown chased that pig for two hours, until it finally died of a heart attack. Tío William later joked that he almost couldn't bring himself to eat it—almost.

We children were also told the ancient story of Mary and Joseph's journey to Bethlehem, where Mary gave birth to Baby Jesus and was visited by the Wise Men. Abuela Ana told us this tale, relating it with such simple faith that I believed she'd probably been there and seen the whole thing.

"Remember, kids," she said, "it's all very well to have fun at Christmastime, to eat and drink and play, but let's never forget the real reason we celebrate at this time of year—to honor the birth of Our Lord and Savior."

But 1961 would be the last year that we would celebrate Noche Buena publicly, because of what happened that night.

Even if we'd known that this was the last one, there was not a thing we would have done differently. The men put up barricades to block the street to traffic. The women set up tables in front of every house and loaded them with food until the legs threatened to buckle. Papa and Tío Cholu had brought back plenty of fresh food from their Tuesday delivery trips to the countryside, and all the women had been saving things so they could outdo themselves with the cooking. I couldn't pass a table without someone grabbing my elbow and sticking some delicious morsel in my mouth. There were no complaints from me. I could usually eat enough for two boys, and that night I ate for three.

Traditionally, the main dishes of the Noche Buena feast were pork, plantains, and *congris*, or black beans and rice. Abuela Ana was a congris specialist. She also made a fabulous pumpernickel bread that I can still taste now if I close my eyes. Mama made white rice, seafood empanadas, and croquettes. Tía Carmen, Tío William's wife, loved to cook yuca, and also to make Cuba libres: Coke with rum and a dash of lime juice. The neighbors brought dessert, such as *panetelas*, a type of cake; *capuchinos*, anisette rolls; *casquitos de guayaba con queso*, or guava shells with cheese; and *churros*, fried bread dough coated with sugar.

Two people were missing that year: Tío William and Carmensita. We felt their absence keenly. In years past, Tío William had hosted many Noche Buena feasts in his massive yard, which could easily accommodate up to thirty tables and still leave room for dancing in the middle. Tío William's nickname was Big Daddy. He wore big rings, drove big cars, and smoked big cigars, and he loved to be generous. When he was running the show, Noche Buena started late in the morning, with people stopping by to socialize and have a bite. This casual visiting went on all day, until at last, when night fell, things got serious. Then a band started up, and people ate, drank, and danced until they were on the verge of collapse. Often, they would fall asleep wherever they could find floor space. It was common for total strangers to show up at this party and be given such a warm welcome that they stayed all night. Politicians and policemen were frequent guests, too—all personal friends of Tío William, one of the most successful businessmen in Cienfuegos.

This was the first year in some time that Tío William hadn't hosted Noche Buena, and it was definitely the first time anyone could remember that Tío had stayed away altogether. He lay in bed with the curtains drawn, suffering in silence over the loss of his little girl. I cast a sad glance at his front door every once in a while. It still felt strange to me that Carmensita was gone forever. My child's mind reeled at the concept of eternity. *When you die, you're dead forever*. But what was forever? A very long time, Papa had told me. Longer than I could hold my breath? Far longer than that. Longer than a year? Way longer.

I couldn't imagine a time longer than a year. In a year, I would be seven, which was very old indeed—too old for me to imagine. Meanwhile, Carmensita, in heaven with the angels, would stay eleven forever. I wondered if she was watching our Noche Buena get-together, wishing she could join us. Was she lonely in heaven, or was she happy because she was with God? God loved children, I knew, but . . . did Carmensita miss me?

Well into the night, the street stayed packed with families, the grownups dancing and drinking and the kids running wild. Rolando, Tito, Luis, and I tore around as if we owned the place—in and out of people's houses, through their yards, eating a little here and a little there, laughing, screaming, reverting to a state of anarchy. No one cared. The adults let us do whatever we wanted. For once, we were free.

Suddenly everyone got very quiet. That was when I realized we had been invaded.

They'd appeared silently, out of nowhere, maybe a half dozen of them: a gang of rough-looking men, strangers to our neighborhood. We could tell by the expressions on their unshaven faces that they had not come for the food. Everything about them was mean-looking, right down to the pointy-tipped shoes on their feet. One minute everyone was having a good time, and the next you could hear the cry of a distant parakeet.

We kids backed away. The bad men began to walk down the street, eyeing everyone with the same contemptuous glare. Then one of them winked at Mama.

"Hey, baby!" he greeted her.

That was all our menfolk needed. Instantly, the gang was surrounded by a lot of very angry Cuban gentlemen, Papa in the middle of them.

"Who do you think you are?" "What are you doing here?" "How dare you behave like that?" Everyone shouted at once.

"Pigs!" shouted the leader of the gang, a man with bad skin and missing teeth. "Worms! Traitors! Back off, or there will be trouble!"

"Trouble!" said Abuelo Julian. He pushed his way to the front of the crowd until he was nose-to-nose with the ringleader. "You say there will be trouble? You got that right! But we didn't start it! We're peaceful people, and we don't want any problems. But if you don't turn around right now and get out of here, trouble is exactly what you'll get!"

No doubt Abuelo believed that no one in his right mind would dare harm an old man. But Abuelo was wrong. The leader planted both his hands on Abuelo's chest and pushed him. Abuelo flew through the air, landing on the pavement. He winced in pain, then rolled over onto his side.

"Abuelo!" I yelled.

"Julian!" shouted Abuela Ana, watching from the sidelines.

"Let's get them!" shouted Tío Sergio, the husband of my *madrina*, or godmother, Magalys. He hauled back and landed a right hook on the man's mouth.

And that was the beginning of the end of Noche Buena.

We smaller kids were pushed behind a table by the women, who then formed a protective wall in front of us. Meanwhile, the men attacked with howls of rage and fury, using fists, feet, elbows, knees, even foreheads. I couldn't believe my eyes. Papa himself was right there in the middle of it, fighting like a warrior from ancient times. My heart swelled with pride as I watched him and I wished I were old enough to fight like that.

Then a new sound erupted, one I couldn't identify. I looked around. It was Tío William, screaming with anger. My godmother had gone to get him. He was in such a hurry to join the fighting men that he was still pulling his pants on over the biggest pair of underwear I'd ever seen. Someone had dared to push his venerable father, and that someone was about to get his due.

I'd heard stories of Tío William's wrath before, mostly from Papa, who had occasionally witnessed it in the workplace—though always in response to a broken tool or carelessly misplaced invoice, never to anything serious. Mama's stories were more dramatic. Tío was the eldest of all her siblings, and once or twice, when he was a young man and she still a little girl, she'd seen him explode in fury. She explained that Tío was slow to anger, but once the feeling peaked, he was like thunder in a summer storm.

Now, hurt to the core by Carmensita's death—for which he blamed the Communists—and filled with a murderous rage at these hoodlums—who were obviously on the Communist payroll, hired to cause trouble—he was living up to all the stories I'd ever heard. Despite my panic and fear, I remember feeling pleased that I was finally getting to see Tío William in action.

Tío dived into the melee and unleashed a barrage of punches. Men fell to the ground, bottles flew through the air and shattered, women screamed. Among them was my dear Abuela Ana, who yelled at her husband of fifty years: "Julian, Julian, don't you see that you are just too old for this?"

"Not too old yet!" I heard Abuelo cry.

Emilio Pérez, my father's best friend, who in my eyes was invincible, stood by, just waiting for an opportunity to get into the fight. Then he saw an opening, and he jumped in. But a lucky punch landed flush on his forehead, and Emilio went down like a sack of wet noodles.

"Emilio, get up, please!" I yelled.

Emilio tried to stand, but his knees had turned to water, and he went back down.

"Emilio is hurt!" I yelled to my cousins, who were watching in horror. "They'll kill him, Papa, help him, please!" I shouted.

Seeing the situation, Papa came to Emilio's rescue and pulled him out of the way. I'd always thought Emilio was the strongest man on our block—even stronger than Tío William—and it depressed me to see him like this.

And then it was over. I couldn't see through the screen of women to find out what happened after that, but the next thing I knew, everyone was shaking hands and apologizing. I even saw Tío William hug one of the thugs. There was nervous laughter, and the bad guys retreated down the block—no doubt because they'd lost the fight. Everyone helped right the tables. Brooms were fetched to sweep up the broken dishes and bottles. Dogs appeared to lap up the ruined meals. My friends and I chattered about the mysterious men. Who were they? Why had they done this? What did they want?

Later, Papa explained to me: "Those thugs were sent by the government to scare us."

"But why?" I asked. "What did we do to them?"

"Nothing. That's not the point. They want us to be scared. They've disrupted our most important feast of the year. They want us to know that they control *everything*." His face was white, and his voice was shaking.

Papa's rage, so rarely glimpsed, was infectious. "I hate them!" I screamed. "I'll kill them all! I'll wring their necks and cut their heads off like a bunch of chickens!"

"Hush! You'll do no such thing," Papa said. "You're still just a boy. You have to learn to think, not just to act. They *want* us to fight back. That way they can arrest us."

"Arrest us for what? They started it!"

"There is no right and wrong here, niño," said Papa. "You have to understand that they don't care about that. All they care about is control. Our beautiful island of Cuba is being run by people who are too stupid to understand anything except brute force. That's what they use to make their point, and then people like us end up getting hurt."

"It's not fair," I said.

"No, it's not. But don't worry, Eduar. Someday these people will get what's coming to them. In the meantime, we have to be smarter than they are, and stay out of trouble."

Papa looked at me for a long and serious moment. It seemed as if he wanted to say something else, but I didn't know what. Later I guessed that he wanted to acknowledge the craziness of the times—to apologize, perhaps, for having brought me into this kind of world, but also to assure me that if I stuck it out long enough, I would see better days. Instead, he just gave me a hug and a slap on the back, and sent me on my way.

More Changes

As the days turned into years, our day-to-day lives became more and more oppressive and difficult. Abuela Ana was spending a lot of time waiting in lines for food, and in March 1962, we were given a *libreta*, a ration book, to use to buy food. The first time I went with Abuela and noticed her holding her libreta, I asked her to read me what was in the book to help pass the time. But she replied that it wasn't a story; the libreta merely told her how much food she was allowed to buy.

"That's silly!" I said. "Why carry around a book if it's no fun to read?"

Abuela gave me a wry glance. "Silly is right," she whispered, but that was all she would say.

We waited in line for hours. I thought that whatever was at the end of it must be something really great. When we finally got to the head of the line, we were handed a chunk of hard bread, some sugar, and a bunch of cans with funny writing on them.

"All this time we wait, and this is what they give us?" I said.

"Ha ha! He's only joking," Abuela said quickly to the person behind the counter. Then she rushed me out of there.

When we were on the sidewalk, she grabbed me by the shoulders and brought her eyes to my level—which for her, since she was so short, merely meant bending over. "Niño," she said, "never, ever, *ever* let them hear you complain."

"Who? Never let *who* hear me complain?"

She looked over her shoulder. There was an armed soldier on the corner, and nearby, on a wall, was a poster of Castro with his big, fluffy beard, a smile plastered across his face. By now I knew the man with the beard was the Voice we heard constantly on the radio and loudspeakers. He was the one in charge now, even of those who had once seemed like gods to me—my parents and grandparents.

"Them," she whispered. "The Communists."

"Why not?"

"Because they could take you away—or, more likely, they would take *me* away. You have to stay quiet, Eduar. Never let them know what you are thinking. *M'entiendes?* Do you understand me?"

I nodded, though I didn't understand at all. But I knew Abuela Ana wasn't playing a game. She seemed scared of something. That frightened me. I'd never seen Abuela afraid. She could wring the neck of a chicken without even flinching, and then cut its head off—*smack!*

"Now let's go home," she said. She grabbed my hand and pulled me along after her, double-time. We didn't stop until we were safely home again.

I once asked Papa what the funny writing on the cans was, and he explained that the cans came from Russia.

"Where is Russia?" I asked.

"Russia is very, very far away," said Papa, "though not quite far enough to suit me."

"Why do they send us this stuff?"

"Because," Papa said wearily, "the Russians are best friends with Fidel."

"If they were really friends with Fidel," I said, "they would give him good food to share with us, wouldn't they?"

Papa stared morosely at the can. "Maybe Fidel does like it," he said. "I wouldn't be surprised."

"You think Fidel is eating this garbage?" Mama said bitterly. "He's eating like a king, while the rest of us starve. He and all his friends."

"Hush," said Papa. "Someone on the street could hear you."

"I don't care!" said Mama.

Then in 1963, just before I turned eight, one of the most civilized customs of Cuban life came to an abrupt end on San Carlos Street.

I lay in bed, in the living room where I slept, listening to the gentle clicking of dominoes from Tía Silvia's front porch next door. This sound was the signal for all within earshot to make their way over to watch the action, or just to chat. I could hear the voices of the adults having a good time. I was supposed to be asleep, but I crept from bed and crouched, unseen, behind a post on our porch. Four men, including Papa, straddled wooden chairs around a table, while more stood, watching and talking. Cigar smoke shrouded their heads like clouds over mountaintops. The women, including Mama, talked all at once, using their hands as well as their mouths, their voices rising whenever they got to a punch line or an important point. Every few minutes, one of them would get up and brew another pot of sweet, potent Cuban coffee and serve it to their husbands in espresso cups. The men would down these in one or two swallows. Fueled by the sugar and caffeine, they could play the game until one or two in the morning.

Mama loved these evenings. Even though she was only going next door, she was dressed as if she were headed for a tony night club, as were the other ladies. That night she wore a brightly colored dress and spritzed herself with heavenly perfume. I could still smell the trail she had left from our porch to Tía Silvia's. Papa eyed her appreciatively, joking about the effect her beauty was having on him. Mama rolled her eyes in mockery. This exchange was always subtle and respectful. Papa, like all the men in my family, was a true Cuban gentleman.

Esther, who was now three, was in bed and asleep, which was where I was supposed to be. From my hiding place on the porch, I listened to the clicking, the talking, the laughter, the jokes and jibes, and the night songs of the insects. I smelled the tropical flowers that bloomed all around, mixed with whiffs of cigar smoke. I felt myself starting to drift off. But then, suddenly, the whole street went black.

"*Apagón!*" a man muttered.

This was the name given to the 11 p.m. blackout imposed by the government to conserve resources. Papa said that wasn't the real reason. Communists simply didn't know how to do anything right, not even run the country's power grids. And the blackened streets made it easier for the roving gangs of thugs.

"Even that fat-cat dictator Batista could keep the lights on all night!" Papa said.

"Oh, who cares? I'll just get a couple of kerosene lamps," said Tía Silvia.

The game continued by lamplight. Finally, too drowsy to stay awake any longer, I snuck back into bed. I would have preferred to be part of the action, but it gave me a warm, comfortable feeling to hear the grownups having a good time—talking, laughing, and singing. In my parents' room, I could hear little Esther's gentle snoring. That, too, was a peaceful sound. For the moment, all was well in Glorytown.

I had just fallen asleep when I was jolted awake by different voices from the street—angry, harsh voices. The merriment on the porch stopped. The gentle sounds were replaced by low mutters of disapproval from my father and the other men.

"Hey! You on the porch!" came a rough voice.

"What do you want?" came the reply, which I recognized as a neighbor's voice. "Why are you bothering us?"

"*We're* bothering *you*? No, I think you've got it backward. You're bothering us, sitting around and yelling at each other like a bunch of monkeys! Look at you people! Do you have nothing better to do than sit around all night?"

I crept out of bed and went to the window. There in the street was another gang of nasty-looking men. Whether they were the same ones from Noche Buena two years ago, I couldn't tell. But it didn't matter. I knew they had the same thing in mind. Fear turned my stomach to water.

"This is our barrio!" our neighbor answered. "We can do what we want. You thugs can't just come here and push us around!"

"What did you call us?" the leader roared.

"Thugs! You know you're thugs. You're scum for hire, that's all! Anyone with five bucks in his pocket could buy you."

"Your wife is for hire! At least, that's what I hear."

I heard a chair falling backward as the man shot to his feet. Instantly, the voices of the other men rose.

"No! Don't do it! He's trying to egg you on, to get you in trouble. Don't do it, man! It won't be a fair fight. You know the government sent them and they've got the police and the army on their side."

"Let me go!" screamed the insulted man. "I'll kill that son of a dog!"

"Bring it on!" jeered the thugs. They stayed in the street, waiting. "Come on! Let's do it! Let's have some action!"

But, instead of fighting as they had on Noche Buena, the party on the porch broke up. Everyone trudged silently home. After sending a few more barbs into the night, loud enough for the entire street to hear, the thugs eventually slunk off, disappointed at not having the chance to fight and promising to come back.

Mama and Papa came into the house a few minutes later. Papa was infuriated. He and Mama were talking and he was trying to keep his voice down, but Esther and I were already awake. The veins in his neck stood out, and he clenched and unclenched his fists, his green eyes snapping. Then Esther came over and climbed into his lap, and his rage melted away as he cuddled her. I was too old for cuddling now—men did not get cuddled. At the age of seven, I considered myself well on the road to manhood. Soon I would be able to take on a whole gang of thugs by myself. I could hardly wait.

"How come you guys didn't kick their butts?" I asked.

"Eduar!" Mama said sharply. "Such language!"

"Because," Papa said wearily, "I would get arrested. So would all the men on San Carlos Street. The army would come and yank us out of our beds. They would take us to prison, and who knows when you would see me again? And how would you eat while I was gone? Who would protect you?"

"But you're not protecting us now!" I yelled. "You're just sitting on the porch like a bunch of scaredy-cats! What's the matter with you guys, anyway? Why don't you teach them a lesson?"

"Eduardo Francisco Calcines, you are going to get the whipping of a lifetime!" Mama said, her voice rising.

"Concha, please," Papa said. "I understand what the boy is saying. He's right to wonder why we don't defend ourselves. What you have to understand, Eduar, is that there are more ways of fighting back than just using your fists. If you refuse to play the game by the only rules they understand, then they can't beat you. See?"

"No," I said, because it seemed to me they were beating us before we even had a chance to play.

"Look at it this way. Do you want Papa to get arrested?"

"No."

"Of course not. That's why we didn't fight them. Who cares about a few insults? Sticks and stones can break my bones, but names can never hurt me."

I had heard that one before, and I thought it was a load of manure. Names *did* hurt—a lot. Especially when they were directed at the people I loved. But I was beginning to understand what Papa was saying. I didn't agree with him—I was too young to grasp the subtleties of the situation. In later years, however, I would remember the wisdom of Papa's words, and I would be grateful for them. For now, it was better to ignore the thugs and pretend nothing was happening.

But something *was* happening. Night after night, the gangs roved up and down San Carlos Street, just waiting for the chance to stomp someone to a pulp and get him sent to prison.

The discussion about our family leaving Cuba was ongoing, and a few nights later, Abuela Ana and Abuelo Julian came over to listen and offer their views, which were always for freedom.

"Go," Abuela said. "Get the children out of this hell. Take them where they will have a chance."

Abuelo said nothing. It seemed from the look on his face, that his heart was breaking. The families closest to him and Abuela were the most serious about leaving. They included Tío William, Tía Carmen, and their two sons; tiny Tía Dinorah and her husband, the bald-headed and hilarious Tío Arturo, and little daughter Cary—their son Arturito was already in America through an arrangement with the Catholic church; wild and crazy Tío Cholu, his gentle wife, Tata, and their five children; the stocky and fiery Tía Aida, her bird-loving husband, Yeyo, and their two sons, my pal Luis and his brother Ernesto; my godmother Magalys, her handsome husband, Sergio, son, Armando, and daughter, Lilly; and, of course, my family: Mama, Papa, Esther, and myself. Including Arturito, that was twenty-seven people in all.

Abuelo and Abuela had seven other children with large families of their own, and they had all decided to stay and wait it out. I knew that my grandparents would never leave Cuba. They had grown too old to start over in America.

My world was disappearing fast. Turmoil swirled around me: death, imprisonment, fear, whispered conversations, hunger, and sleeplessness. I was sliding down a dark hole with nothing to hold on to. Little remained constant. There was Pichilingo, my beloved rooster, and the rooftop in Abuela's yard, where I still believed I would be safe no matter what. But everything else was becoming unfamiliar.

Stories to Ease the Pain

To fill the nighttime hours, Papa told Esther and me stories of when he was a boy, and I loved to escape into his world.

"Once upon a time, niños, I was nothing more than a *guajirito*, a poor little country boy. I was the sixteenth child born to my mother," Papa would tell us, "and I was the youngest boy. When my papa died, I had to drop out of the third grade and go to work."

"You did?" I asked. I had heard this story before, but I always pretended it was the first time.

"Yes. But I never felt sorry for myself. It was my lot in life, and my mother, your abuela Petra, pushed me along as well as my brothers and sisters, never allowing any one of us to feel sorry for ourselves. She was a strong and strict woman who smoked cigars and raised all of us by herself; we all became good men and women with families of our own. I'm sorry we didn't visit her very often and you didn't really get to know her before she died last year. You know something?" Papa asked. "Most of us stayed here in Cienfuegos because that was your abuela Petra's wish. We never had much while growing up, but now look at me—I have a beautiful young wife, a healthy little family, and a nice house to live in. I am truly a real king."

"Does that mean I'm a prince?"

"Yes, it does!" Papa declared, pleased with this notion. "Eduar, you are the prince of Glorytown! And Esther is the princess!"

Esther and I grinned at each other. We hadn't known we were royalty.

Story time wasn't limited to the evenings. In summer, when the heat was so thick you could have spread it on a piece of pumpernickel bread, Papa often came home from work for lunch and an afternoon siesta. Esther and I would pile next to him in bed as he tried to rest, begging him to tell us just one story.

"Let me sleep!" he'd groan. "It's hot, and I'm tired! I've been driving since before dawn!"

Papa and Tío Cholu got up at three or four in the morning during the summer so they could make their first rounds before the heat set in. By lunchtime, they had already put in an eight-hour day, and they had more work ahead of them in the afternoon.

But we were merciless.

"Just one!" I'd beg. "Come on, Papa! Please! Tell us about when your papa died and you came to Cienfuegos!"

"All right, all right! Let me see . . . Well, I remember that terrible day all too well," he said. "That heartless plantation owner threw us all out of our house, if you can imagine someone doing a thing like that."

"Why did he do it?"

"Because he was greedy, and all he cared about was money."

"Couldn't your brothers work on the plantation?"

"The plantation owner needed my father's expertise," said Papa, "and when he died, the owner wanted to replace him with someone else. None of my brothers had my father's experience in the fields. So he told us we had to go."

"Then what did you do?"

"You know what we did!"

"Tell us anyway!"

"We walked all the way to Cienfuegos, and when we got here, I dropped out of school forever."

That line was one of my favorite parts of the story.

"I want to drop out of school, too!" I said. Already, though I had only finished third grade, school and I had a tumultuous relationship. God did not make me to sit still in a classroom, I believed, and my marks were unfortunate proof of that.

But Papa said, "No, Eduar. I had no choice. You do. And if I ever hear you talk about dropping out of school again, I will burn your bottom, m'entiendes?"

"Yes, Papa. Why did you have to drop out, then?"

"Because I had to get a job."

"What job?"

"My first job was delivering bread. Your tío Amado and I got up at three in the morning and worked until dark. I didn't mind. I liked to work. And if I didn't have that bread route, I never would have met Ritica Suares del Villar—better known as Ritica la Cubanita."

"Who is that?"

"Oh, Ritica was famous. She was really old when I met her. She had a little farm with a few cows, which the government had given her as a reward for her patriotic service. She took a liking to me, so she gave me extra work cleaning out the stalls. And then, one day, she started telling me stories."

"What about?"

"The War of Independence against the Spanish."

This was another favorite part for me. Anything to do with war was interesting—as long as it wasn't happening right here and now.

Papa settled back into his pillow, giving up on sleep for the time being.

"It happened a long time ago, when Ritica was just a young woman," he said. "She used to feed the soldiers and make them bandages, and she also helped make the first Cuban flag. I called Ritica my 'second mother,' because my own mother had so many other children to look after she barely had any time for me. I spent a lot of time with Ritica."

"Is she still alive?"

"No, but she made it to one hundred and two," Papa said.

"What! How did she manage that?"

"By believing in God, country, and family," said Papa, rolling over. "And by letting her papa take his naps in the afternoons. Now run along and let me sleep!"

"But wait, Papa. Was Ritica the reason you didn't become a Communist?"

Papa looked at me, his gaze steady and serious.

"Niño, remember what I just told you about what Ritica believed in?"

"Yes, Papa. She believed in God, country, and family."

"Well, so do I. The Communists don't believe in anything, except power and control. That's why I didn't become a Communist."

"Tell us one more story, Papa," Esther said. "Tell us 'Dos Gardenias'!"

"Concha, will you come get these two?" Papa yelled.

"No!" Mama said from the next room. "I want to hear how you tell this one!"

"Ah, I'm surrounded," Papa said, rolling once more onto his back and cushioning his head on his arms. "So, you want to hear 'Dos Gardenias' again?"

"Yes!"

"Okay, here it comes. Once, a long time ago, before either of you was born, I overheard Mama say to her sister—"

"Which sister?" Esther asked.

"Tía Violeta," Papa said, pulling her nose. "So that day I overheard Mama say to Tía Violeta that she was going to go to the beach. Well, when I heard that, I got my brother—"

"Which brother?" I asked.

"Tío Amado, as if you didn't know. And I said, 'Listen, Amado, how about we follow along?' Of course he agreed, because he knew how in love with your mama I was. Did you hear that, Conchita?"

"Yes, Felo," Mama said, sounding pleased. "Keep going."

"You could rent rowboats at this place," Papa continued, "and Mama and Tía Violeta went out in one boat. So I said to Amado, 'Let's go out in another one.' And we rowed and rowed."

"Are you a fast rower?" I asked.

"The fastest in all of Cuba," said Papa.

"Wow!" I said.

"Why did you row after her?" Esther asked. "Were you trying to catch her?"

"Yes! Because she was so beautiful, and I was in love with her. Did you hear that, Concha?"

"Yes, Felo," Mama said. "Keep going."

"And so finally we got up to her boat, and I could see how the wind was moving through her hair, and the sun was making her skin glow, and her eyes were sparkling—just like the surface of the sea, which was so beautiful that day, like a million diamonds! And that, my niños, was when I really fell in love with her, hook, line, and sinker!"

"And so what did you do?" I asked.

"And so I did what any red-blooded Cuban man would do in my situation. I sang her a love song!"

"Yay! Sing it! Sing it!" cried Esther.

Papa cleared his throat, then burst into song:

Dos gardenias para ti,
con ellas quiero decir
te quiero, te adore, mi vida.
Ponles toda tu atención
porque son tu corazón y el mio.

This was a poetic and romantic song, which translates:

Two gardenias for you,
with them I want to say
I love you, I adore you, my darling.
Give them all of your attention
Because they are your heart and mine.

At that point, Esther and I burst into mad applause, and Mama came in to reward Papa for his performance with a big kiss.

"Did I get the story right?" he asked Mama.

"Close enough, Felo," she said. "Close enough."

I always loved Papa's stories of the old days. I would have liked to meet someone as interesting as Ritica la Cubanita, but the only old ladies I knew were Abuela, whose stories I had heard a million times, and La Natividad, the crazy old lady at the end of San Carlos Street who screeched at every small boy she saw and practiced black magic in her house. It was whispered that even the C.D.R. lady on our block was afraid of La Natividad. There was no way I was going to knock on her door. I would probably get turned into a bat for my trouble.

Tío William's Arrest

My parents saw it as their job to protect us from the harsh realities of the Revolution. Of course, Esther and I sensed their anxiety, anyway. But I had learned by now that it had nothing to do with whether or not I was a good boy. Rather, it was all about Fidel and his minions. What would they do next? We could only wait and see. There was no way to prepare for the challenges life was going to throw at us, and that made even me feel helpless. Then early in 1965, the unthinkable happened.

One morning there was a commotion in Abuela Ana and Abuelo Julian's living room. I was up on the roof, practicing my birdcalls on Pichilingo and Pepe, another friend of mine, who happened to be a mockingbird. I climbed down the avocado tree to see what was going on, only to find my grandparents consoling Tía Carmen, who was in tears. Tío William had been formally accused of conspiring to assist anti-Castro rebels. He'd been arrested by the police that morning and taken to jail.

Tío William stood out as a target. He'd been a successful capitalist, which was suddenly the worst thing anyone could be. He'd even been president of the Cienfuegos Lion's Club. He played a pivotal role in supporting his extended family, feeding not only his own wife and children, but his parents as well. He was my father's employer, which meant we also depended upon Tío. The same was true of Tío Cholu, who had four children of his own. Many other family members depended in smaller ways on his generosity. Besides, we all loved Tío William. If something bad happened to him, it happened to all of us.

The charges were serious, and we were very worried. But then Abuelo Julian contacted an old friend, a lawyer who was now serving as a prosecutor for Castro's "killing courts." We called them by that name because they sentenced so many innocent people to death. The accused weren't even allowed to have legal representation. They were charged, summoned to court, found guilty, and either sent to jail or stood up against a wall and shot.

Again, we got lucky. This lawyer friend became our angel. He helped to find Tío William guilty of a lesser offense, condemning him to prison for only two years. My mother sighed with relief. But my father once again swelled with anger that he could barely hold in.

"Why should we consider ourselves lucky that William is going to jail for two years?" he said, disgusted. "Why should he go to prison at all? Before the Revolution, he was a model citizen. Now he's a criminal? It's insane!"

Probably because of this powerful lawyer friend, Tío was allowed to keep his distribution company open while he was in prison. But for how long? Another day, week, or year? We knew that at any moment, the government could step in, close the whole thing down, and confiscate everything: the fleet of trucks, the tools to repair them, the metal cylinders the gas was delivered in, the building itself. Who was going to say no? My father told me that all over the country, business owners like Tío were losing everything they owned. The Communists were nationalizing everything, he said. When I asked Papa what "nationalize" meant, he said, "It means they're stealing in the name of the state."

I also heard Papa tell Mama that Tío could be away a lot longer than two years, depending on whether or not he was considered "rehabilitated as a member of the Revolution."

"How can robbing a man of everything he has worked for, everything he holds dear, possibly win him over to your cause?" Papa raged.

Mama said nothing. What was there to say?

Tío's prison sentence struck terror in me. The grownups tried not to talk about it in front of the children, but I heard enough to know it was bad. Once, I listened as Papa and my uncles talked about how the prison system operated on snitching. If you ratted someone out, you would be rewarded by the guards, but you would be hated by the other prisoners. If you didn't rat, the guards could be brutal, but the prisoners would respect you.

That fall, Esther started kindergarten and I began fifth grade. I walked her to Mariana Grajales Elementary School with my own group consisting of Rolando and Tito—who, even though they were sons of Communists, were still allowed to play with me—and my *primo*, or cousin, Luis, born one month before me. Tito was about ten months older than Rolando, but we were all in the same grade. These three had always walked to school with me, and we formed a phalanx whose job was to keep each other safe. Esther, our princess, now walked in the middle, protected by all of us.

"Calcines!" said Tito one day as we headed to school. "How come your dad doesn't join the Communist Party, like our dad?"

"What!" I said. "The Communists locked him up in that theater for three whole days during the Bay of Pigs. They took away Tío William. They hired thugs to make everyone's lives miserable. Why would he want anything to do with them?"

"If he was a Communist, he would have a job for life," Rolando explained.

"You don't have any more than we do," I retorted. "You still have to carry the same stupid ration books as everyone else, don't you? And don't you get stuck eating the same canned horse meat from Russia as the rest of us?"

"Yeah! And you have to go to those marches all the time!" Luis chimed in.

"Aiee, I hate those marches!" Tito said, rolling his eyes.

"Me, too," Rolando said. "They're endless! And the blisters!"

"And those speeches!" said Tito. "How many more times is Castro going to promise us that things will get better tomorrow? Why don't they just get better, already?"

"Because," Rolando explained to his brother, "the worms who don't agree with the Revolution are holding the rest of us back. That's what Dad says, anyway."

"That's a bunch of crap," I said. "It's the Communists' own fault that nothing works and nobody has enough food. They just don't want to admit it."

"That's right," said Luis. "No one is trying to stop the Communists from making Cuba a better place. They're just too stupid to get it right."

"Tell it like it is, primo," I said. Luis and I slapped each other's palms.

"Ah, whatever," said Rolando. "Talking about politics gives me a headache."

"Me, too," said Tito.

"You know what I miss? Ketchup," I said.

"Me, too!" said Luis.

"Us, too!" said Tito. "Man, if I had a bottle of ketchup, I would drink the whole thing right now."

"Gross! I would eat it little by little, to cover up the taste of that horse meat they give us," I said.

"What's ketchup?" asked Esther.

"You see? This is how bad things are! My poor sister doesn't even know what ketchup is!"

"You know what I miss?" said Luis. "Gum!"

Tito, Rolando, and I groaned. It had been so long since I'd had a piece of gum I'd forgotten all about it.

"What's gum?" Esther asked.

"What's gum, she says!" Luis howled. "Oh, man, Esther hasn't ever had gum!"

"Gum is this great stuff you stick in your mouth and chew but don't swallow," I explained. We rounded the corner, approaching the school. I kept my voice down, lest anyone hear me wax eloquent on yet another failure of the Communist government: Cuban children's lack of American chewing gum. "It gets all soft in your mouth, and you can blow bubbles with it, and it stays tasty forever!"

"Well, that depends on what kind you get," Tito reminded me.

"That's true, Calcines," said Rolando. "Some kinds of gum last longer than others."

"Me, I like Juicy Fruit!" said Luis. "Oh, man, what I wouldn't give for a stick of that right now!"

"Juicy Fruit is okay," I allowed. "But I like Big Red better."

"Will you get me some gum someday, Eduardito?" Esther asked.

"Of course I will," I assured her. "I promise."

"Where are you going to get it?" Luis asked. "Get me some, too!"

"Yeah, Calcines!" said Tito. "I want to get in on some of this gum action."

"No," I said. "You guys can take care of yourselves. Esther has never had gum. I want her to know what it's like. It's the best stuff in the whole world!"

"Good morning, boys. Good morning, Esther," said the principal, a blond woman who stood outside every morning to greet the children. "What is the best stuff in the whole world, Eduardo?"

"Nothing, ma'am," I said. "We were just talking about—uh—"

"About pumpernickel bread," said Luis quickly.

"Ah, yes. Well, have a good day, and study hard for the glory of the Revolution!" she said, motioning us inside.

We boys said goodbye to one another, promising to meet in front of the school after class was over, as usual. I walked Esther to her room, but before she went in, something possessed me to lean forward and whisper in her ear: "Esther, I promise, someday I'm going to get you all the gum you can chew."

Esther smiled. For a moment I wished I'd chosen my words more carefully. Would I be able to live up to my promise? But her faith in me was touching, and it moved me to make yet another one.

"I'm going to take us to America," I whispered. "That's where the best chewing gum is. Ketchup, too. We'll have all the food we want, and no one will bother us anymore. Don't tell anybody, though, or we'll get in trouble. Okay?"

"Okay!" Esther whispered back. There was no doubt in her mind that her big brother was going to do what he said. She squeezed my hand and gave me a peck on the cheek. Then she turned and went into her classroom, and I went on my way to mine.

Well, I had dug a big hole for myself now. There was not a Calcines yet who had failed to keep his word. I was committed. Now the only question was: How would I do it?

Frankly, I had no idea. But I was sure that something would turn up.

In the meantime, it was back to the same old thing—keeping my head down and making sure I stayed out of trouble. So, with a heavy heart, I went into my own classroom and sat at my desk, resigning myself to another day of Communist propaganda from our teacher.

149901

The government's thirty-day allotment of food rations was barely enough to keep one person alive, let alone a whole family, so by the end of each month we'd often run out of rations. This meant we had to scrounge whatever we could on the black market along with whatever fruit was in season that we could find on the trees. We were luckier than others, though, because of Papa's trips to the country on Tuesdays and because Mama was resourceful and always managed to come up with one meal a day. When our bellies rumbled, she would hand Esther and me a piece of hard bread and a cup of sugar water. "No complaining!" Mama would say, but I could see in her eyes that she knew the situation was pathetic.

If it had been possible for our parents to sacrifice any more, they would have. But it wasn't possible. They ate only as much as they needed to stay alive, leaving the rest for us. Most of Abuela Ana's chickens had been slaughtered. There were just a few scrawny survivors now, plus the indomitable Pichilingo. Someday, I worried, it would be his turn for the pot. I knew Abuela was saving him for truly desperate times. But I couldn't bear to think of eating my old friend, so I prayed that Fidel would die before my rooster lost his head.

The food situation was even worse for my classmate Tito Bemba, whom we all called Quco. I had always liked Quco. He had the biggest pair of lips in Glorytown, and he loved to pucker up and chase the girls around, threatening to kiss them. But he was one of eight children, and I could always tell when his family's rations had run out, because he would sit quietly on the playground instead of playing, in order to conserve energy.

"Quco!" I said to him one day. "What's up? Why are you just sitting here?"

"Aiee, Calcines, man." He rolled his eyes. "If I stand up too fast, I get dizzy."

"You're that hungry?"

"You have no idea, Calcines. We haven't had anything to eat for two days. Not a bite."

"Listen, you come home with me after school," I said. "Maybe I can get you a little something."

"Forget it, Calcines. It's nice of you, but I don't want to take food out of your family's mouths."

"No, really. It's okay. Mama always manages to come up with something."

Quco finally agreed. I took him home to my place, and we went into the kitchen, where Mama was mixing brown sugar with water—about the only two things we had plenty of. As usual, she greeted me with a big kiss, and she offered Quco a pleasant hello, asking how his family was doing.

"Mama," I said, "Quco hasn't had anything to eat in two days. Can we give him something?"

"Of course," Mama said. She went to the freezer and pulled out a tray. "This is all I have right now, boys, but you are welcome to it. It's *durofrio*."

Durofrio, literally "hard and cold," was one more trick Mama had come up with to stave off our hunger pangs. It was nothing but brown sugar water, frozen into cubes. But it filled the belly for a little while, and the sugar gave us a little energy boost, though often afterward I would feel even more tired than before. I was disappointed that this was all we had to offer, but Quco's family didn't even have a freezer. His eyes lit up as though he'd just been invited to a banquet.

"Thanks, Señora Calcines!" he said, and promptly helped himself to a piece of ice. I did, too. We stood in the kitchen, sucking on our durofrios and chatting with Mama, until Quco felt a little better. He thanked her and said he would be on his way.

"Wait, Quco," said Mama. She got a clean kitchen towel and wrapped up a bunch of durofrios for him to take home. "Hurry and get these back to your house before they melt," she instructed him. "I'm sure all those brothers and sisters of yours will want a little something to nibble on."

Quco's eyes got big and misty.

"Thank you, Señora Calcines," he said. "Thank you very much. And God bless you." He grabbed the towel, said, "See you tomorrow, Calcines," and scurried out the door.

Mama watched him go. Then she shook her head and went back to her work.

One day I heard my mother and a neighbor whispering.

"Suicide. He committed suicide!" the neighbor said.

"It's the hunger, the propaganda, the executions. We're not even allowed to go to church or play dominoes. What do you expect?"

"He couldn't handle the pressure. Every day, he thought he might be arrested for no reason at all. And why stay alive just to go into the army and get killed? How can we all live like this?"

Surely it was gossip, I thought. But then over the next few months I began to hear Mama, Abuela, and Madrina Magalys whisper more and more names of the dead men. *Hugo, Ernesto, Gerardo.* I knew them all! They were only boys. I could see their faces in my mind, and they began to haunt me. Suicide is a sin, but if God was watching what was going on in Cuba, surely he would understand. I thought of the boys as martyrs to the cause of freedom, and in my daydreams they took on a heroic status. It required guts to kill yourself.

A lot of young men were choosing suicide over being drafted into Castro's brutal army. Suicide was not a coward's way out if one had no other choice. It was the ultimate act of defiance against the government, a reminder that Castro could never really control the people the way he thought he could. His armies and thugs might take away our livelihood, our food, our peace of mind, but they could never touch our souls. I prayed that the boys who killed themselves would find peace in the next life.

Even though I was still a kid, in a few short years I would be fifteen, old enough to be drafted. It could take that long for us to get permission to leave Cuba. The lesson of thc suicides was not lost on my parents. If we were going to get out, we would have to start making plans now. Otherwise, it might be too late.

One night toward the end of August 1966, I was listening to Papa and Mama talk as they lay in bed. I could hear every word through the wall, and I remained still and silent, absorbing everything.

"We have two choices," Papa said. "We can do it the legal way, or the illegal way."

The legal way, I knew, meant applying to the government for an exit visa. But what about the illegal way?

"Well, I can tell you right now that I am not putting my children on an inner tube and pushing them off into the ocean!" Mama said, tears in her voice. "You know what the military does to those people they catch trying to leave!"

So that was what she meant. Even I knew all about the people who tried to get to America across the Straits of Florida, clinging to anything that floated. With American soil a tantalizing ninety miles from Havana, it wasn't hard to see why so many people made the attempt to escape the island prison. The Gulf Stream passed Cuba and went right by Miami, and it was tempting to believe that one could get to America in a few short hours. As long as the Cuban navy or the sharks didn't get you, and as long as you didn't get caught up in a storm or somehow end up floating in the wrong direction, you could make it. It had been done.

But nobody knew how many people had died trying. The government wasn't exactly forthcoming about how many escapees they murdered every month, but the stories I heard whispered on the streets were chilling. When the navy came across boat people, regardless of how many or how old they were, they all got the same treatment—a burst of machine-gun fire. Then the sharks got a free lunch.

"Shh, Concha," Papa soothed her. "Yes, I know. And I will not put my family in such a position."

"I would do it if there was no other way." Mama sobbed. "I would. But as long as we have a chance to get out safely, we have to take it. For the sake of the children."

"Yes," Papa agreed. "For the sake of the children."

"We'll do it, then?"

"Yes. I'll go tomorrow and make the application."

Mama was quiet for several moments.

"I'm glad."

"Me, too."

"But I'm scared."

"Me, too."

I thought I knew why Mama was scared. I was scared, too, and as I lay in bed I had to fight to keep the panic from rising in my chest. People who applied for exit visas were subject to a kind of public ridicule that could, and did, break even the strongest wills. I had seen it on the playground. The children of those who had declared their discontent were called *gusanos*—worms—and were beaten and tormented constantly by the other kids. I never participated in this bullying. It was mostly the children of the Communists who did. Rolando and Tito stayed out of it as well. They said it gave them a bad taste in their mouths to see the way those kids were treated.

But the worst of it was that even the teachers got in on the act. The previous spring, I'd witnessed a terrible thing. A boy whose parents had recently applied for an exit visa was getting beaten up on the playground by three or four bigger kids. A teacher, a young man I didn't know, walked over to where the beating was taking place. Those of us who were watching expected him to stop it and punish the bullies. But instead, to my astonishment, he said, "That's right, boys! That's what happens to those who doubt the power of the Revolution! If you don't like this treatment, you little worm, then maybe you should go home and tell your father to reconsider!" And with that, he walked away.

If Papa appied for a visa, this was going to be my fate when school started. I knew that their decision was not easy for Mama and Papa, especially because the consequences of it would be felt by all of us.

Well, almost all of us. Lying in the darkness, I gritted my teeth and made a silent vow: anyone who laid a hand on my sister was going to get the living daylights knocked out of him, whether teacher or student. No one was going to hurt Esther as long as I was alive.

The next day, true to his word, Papa went to see an immigration representative and told him the Calcines family of San Carlos Street wanted to leave the country. When he came back, he was a changed man.

"Did you do it?" Mama asked, anxious.

"Yes, I did it," he said. He showed us a piece of paper with a number on it: 149901.

"What's that?" I asked.

"It's our visa number," said Papa.

"What do we do with it?"

"The immigration people take all the numbers and put them in a big bowl," Papa explained. "Then, every day, they draw a few numbers, and they send those people a telegram."

"What will the telegram say?"

"It will say that we have been granted permission to leave the country, and we have one week to get our affairs in order. Then we have to be at the airport at such and such a time, and we'll . . . we'll get on an airplane, and we'll . . ." Papa's voice began to falter as the import of what he was saying sank in. The significance was so huge, it was difficult to utter. "We'll fly to Florida," he said. "It takes no time at all. We'll be there in forty-five minutes. And then we'll be free."

"Well, how long until they draw our number?" I demanded.

"Eduar, we don't know, and there's no point in asking," Mama said. "Don't pester us about this. They call it when they call it. It's up to them."

"But will it be next week?"

"It might be next week or next year. Or two years."

"Oh, there's no way it will take that long," Papa said with confidence. "A year, at most."

"Still, it's better just to forget about it and go on with business as usual. That way, when it happens, it will come as a surprise." She glanced at Papa and gave him an uncertain smile. "It will be like the best birthday present you've ever gotten," she said. "Times ten."

"Times a hundred," said Papa.

"But how do we know it's not rigged?" I said. "How do we know they're really drawing them fairly? Maybe they only pick the numbers they want! We could be waiting forever!"

"Eduar," Papa said, "I'm telling you, just do your best to forget about it."

Forget about it? Were my parents crazy? How on earth was I supposed to forget about something like this? It was impossible.

"What about Abuela and Abuelo?" Esther wanted to know. "Are they coming, too?"

I already knew the answer, but I didn't say anything. Papa and Mama exchanged another long look. Mama clamped her lips together and opened her eyes wide, staring up at the ceiling. I knew why she did this—to keep from crying.

"No," Papa said. "Abuela and Abuelo will stay here, along with those members of our family who have chosen to remain in Cuba."

"But won't they miss us?"

"Of course they'll miss us," Mama said.

"Can we come and visit them whenever we want?" Esther pressed.

She was still only five, and the complexities of what we were facing were beyond her. At my advanced age of ten, I felt I understood all about it. "No, we can't," I said. "We won't ever see them again for the rest of our lives. Or anybody else from Glorytown! We have to leave here and never come back, all because of that stupid monkey Fidel!"

"Eduar! Your mouth!" Papa said. "Concha, close the door!"

Mama got up and shut the front door.

"How many times do I have to tell you to keep your voice down when we are speaking of these things?" Papa said. "If anyone had been listening, we would all be in big trouble!"

"I'm sorry, Papa," I said.

"Listen, children. This is a very hard burden for kids as young as you to bear, but we have no choice. For now, I'm going to give you some strict rules to follow until the day we get that telegram, no matter when it comes. Especially you, Eduar. Listen carefully. If anyone tries to start a fight, get away from him. Don't hit back, whatever you do. Niño, from now on, you are to stay close to home, do you hear me? And, Esther, I don't want you leaving the house except to go to school, when it starts. You stay safe with Mama. Do you understand?"

"Yes, Papa," we said.

"Good," Papa said.

He'd finally taken the step he had dreamed of for so long, but instead of looking happy, he now looked worried.

The government followed up right away and sent an officer to our house to take inventory of all our possessions. They did this because when it came time to leave we were only allowed to take a few things, so most of what was considered ours was by law now considered property of the state. The government wanted to make sure nothing disappeared between now and when we left.

Gusanos

School started a few days later, in September. That morning, after a breakfast of sugar water, hard bread, and half an egg from one of Abuela's chickens, Esther and I waited on the corner for Tito, Rolando, and Luis, as usual. Since Papa applied for the visa I had stayed close to home and had been afraid that Tito and Rolando wouldn't be allowed to associate with me anymore. But they came out of their house right on time, and a moment later Luis appeared. I breathed a sigh of relief. Maybe Tito and Rolando didn't know about the visa yet; maybe no one at school did. The four of us, plus Esther, started walking to school.

Tito was the first to speak.

"So, your father really went ahead and did it!" he said in awed tones.

"Yup." The fact that Tito knew about it meant that the whole school did, too. I'd been hoping for a grace period, but I could see now I wasn't going to get one.

"Are you afraid?" he asked.

"Nah," I lied.

"When do you think your visa will come?" Rolando asked.

"It will come when it comes," I said. "My parents told me not to ask."

"I wish my parents would decide to take us to America!" said Luis. "What do you think it's going to be like, Eduardo?"

"How should I know? I'm not even there yet," I said.

Apparently our becoming dissenters had given me new status in the eyes of my friends. I was now regarded as an authority on all things American, and as we walked to school, they asked me a dozen questions, for which I had no more answers than I'd ever had.

Their questions proving futile, the boys turned to wild speculation on what my life as a Yankee was going to be like.

"I bet you're gonna get a girlfriend with blue eyes and blond hair!" declared Rolando.

"Yeah, and you're gonna go to baseball games and eat hot dogs," said Luis wistfully. "And apple pie! Americans eat apple pie every day!"

"What's a hot dog?" Esther asked. "We won't have to eat dogs in America, will we, *hermano*?"

"No, no," I said crossly. Ordinarily I would have found this funny, but the tension was getting the better of me. "Hot dogs are like sausages. You eat them in buns."

"Oh, man! With ketchup and mustard!" said Rolando, clutching his stomach.

"And relish!" said Tito.

"What is it with you guys? Stop talking about food! You're killing me!" said Luis.

"Well," I said as the school came into sight, "here we are."

"Listen, Calcines," said Rolando uncomfortably. "I just want to tell you . . . if the other kids start in on you, you know, because of your visa thing . . ."

"Yeah?"

"Well . . . don't hold it against us if we don't say anything, all right? We don't want to get into trouble with the Communists. Our dad doesn't mind us hanging out with you, but he doesn't need any extra trouble, either."

"Thanks a lot," I said. "Some friends you are. If someone was ganging up on you, I wouldn't just stand there and do nothing! I'd fight!"

"Don't be like that, Eduardo," said Tito. "You know it's more complicated than that."

"Yeah," said Rolando. "Way more."

"Don't worry, Calcines," said Luis, his voice full of scorn. "I'm gonna back you up one hundred percent, 'cause you're my primo. And if these scared little girls don't want to jump in, then that's their problem. Maybe they're afraid they're gonna break a nail."

"I don't care about myself," I said. "I can take care of myself. There is no one my age in Cienfuegos whose butt I can't kick to the moon and back, you hear me? But I'll tell you one thing right now. If you guys see anyone doing anything to Esther, and you don't help her, so help me God, I will wring your necks with my bare hands. Understand?"

Tito and Rolando looked at each other.

"Don't worry," Rolando said. "We won't let anything happen to Esther."

"You better not," I said.

"Is someone going to hurt me?" Esther asked.

"No, hermana," I said. "Luis and I will protect you."

I could see by their expressions that the brothers were feeling guilty. But I didn't care about their problems. I was worried about my own.

I took Esther to her classroom and then walked into my own. Trouble started immediately.

My teacher that year was Señora Felicia. Like all the other teachers in Cuba, she had been selected because of her loyalty to the Communists. We all knew that Fidel thought of schools as indoctrination centers. When he took over the island, one of the first things he did was abolish the traditional education system. He replaced it with a curriculum based on the glories of Communism, including lots of lessons on the Soviet Union, which according to our teachers was just one level below heaven. All the schools were renamed after Communist heroes. And from kindergarten on, we had our heads filled with propaganda about the evils of Yankee imperialism and the wonders of the Soviet Union. By the sixth grade, I had already seen through all the nonsense they tried to shove down our throats. So had my friends. We learned how to tune it out.

But teachers behaved like government authorities. You had to be as careful of them as you were of the police, because if they overheard you say something against the Revolution, they could report you—and your whole family could get into trouble.

I walked into Señora Felicia's sixth grade classroom and took a seat in the back of the room. I hoped that no one would notice me. A few kids looked my way and exchanged whispers, but that was it. So far, so good.

Then Señora Felicia entered the room. "Everyone, stand up!" she commanded.

"Good morning, Señora!" we chanted.

"Sit down!"

We sat down.

"Calcines! Not you, you rockhead! Stand up!"

I did so. My face was already burning, and my knees had begun to tremble.

Señora Felicia was a short, stocky, dark woman with plump cheeks, pointed eyebrows, and cat's-eye glasses. She used her eyebrows to frightening effect, arching them and staring me down. I felt as if a chunk of ice was growing in my stomach.

"I want everyone to take a good look at Calcines," said Señora Felicia. "Because this is what a worm looks like. A traitorous, disgusting worm. Look, everyone!"

A few of the kids snickered. Most of the others seemed just as uncomfortable as I was. But that was shortly to change.

"Why don't you tell us, Calcines, exactly what your problem is?" the teacher said. "Why is it your father thinks he knows better than our leader? Does Rafael Calcines have a law degree, like El Comandante? Does he think, perhaps, that he is the smartest man in Cuba?"

"No, ma'am," I mumbled.

"Speak up! No, ma'am, what?"

"No, ma'am, my father does not think he is the smartest man in Cuba, ma'am," I said, a little louder.

"We have one word for people like you, Calcines!" the teacher crowed. "And we all know what that word is, don't we, everyone!"

"Gusano," said a few of my classmates. Worm.

"Louder! Everyone!"

"Gusano!" roared the class.

"That's right! Everyone, stand up and tell Mr. Calcines what you think!"

The students stood up. I stood, too, my head bowed, fists clenched, trying to control myself.

"Now, let's hear it, nice and loud! Gusano!"

"Gusano! Gusano! Gusano!" chanted the kids. Egged on by this so-called educator, their voices grew with enthusiasm, and they began to laugh. "Calcines is a gusano!"

"Excellent!" came a new voice from the door. Everyone turned to see the principal standing in the doorway, a pleased expression on her face. "Señora Felicia, I am happy to see that you are instilling the proper values in your students."

"Thank you, principal," said Señora Felicia.

"Calcines!" said the principal. "I have one thing to say to you."

Everyone waited. The only sound was my labored breathing.

"Get out of our country at once! We don't need you," she said. "Then there will be one less worm that our revolutionary government will be forced to re-educate."

I couldn't help myself. The tears began to stream down my cheeks. I closed my eyes and gritted my teeth.

"You may continue with your lesson," said the principal to my teacher. "I only hope that having a worm in your classroom is not too much of a distraction for the other students." And with that, she turned and walked away.

"Take your seats, everyone," said Señora Felicia, looking smug. "You, too, Calcines. And let me tell you something right now. For the rest of the school year, I don't want to hear a single word out of you. Not even to ask permission to use the bathroom. Understand? You can just sit there and keep your mouth shut. Now, let us begin with our geography lesson. Who can point to Moscow on the map?"

We were released onto the playground at lunchtime—or, rather, what should have been lunchtime, except that in this glorious workers' paradise everyone was starving. Almost immediately, I was surrounded by a gang of four boys. The ringleader was a boy I knew well, having gone to school with him since we were five. I had never had a problem with him before, but now he sneered at me.

"Put 'em up!" he said. "Let's see what a worm fights like."

I knew I could have taken any one of those clowns, or even two of them. But I remembered what my papa said.

"If you cowards had to face me in a fair fight," I began—but before I could finish, a fist came crashing into my nose. I fell, blood spurting down my face and chest. Howls and jeers arose from my tormentors.

"What was that you were saying, worm?" one of them taunted me. "Something about us being cowards?"

Other children gathered around to watch the action. The pain in my nose was bad, but the emotional pain was worse. And worst of all was that I couldn't defend myself.

"Hey! Why don't you little girls pick on someone your own size!" came a familiar voice.

I looked up to see Quco Bemba standing over me, his fists clenched. I knew he wouldn't have the strength for a real fight. But he and I locked eyes, and I saw that his face was full of fierce determination. Perhaps he would collapse afterward, but right now, Quco was the only friend I had.

Then something magnificent happened. Three more familiar faces appeared next to Quco: Tito, Rolando, and Luis.

"Back off," Tito told my tormentors. "Or I'm going to rip your intestines out and wrap them around your neck."

"What are you sticking up for him for?" demanded the ringleader. "You're not going soft on us, are—"

He didn't get a chance to finish his sentence, either. Tito drove his fist into the boy's stomach. He doubled over, gasping for air.

"Don't mess with the boys from San Carlos Street," Tito advised him as he writhed on the ground, trying to breathe. "Worm or no, Communist or no, Calcines is one of us, and if you touch him again, I'm gonna—"

"What's going on here?" came an adult voice.

It was a young male teacher. "Did this cowardly worm dare to raise a hand against you, boys?"

"He didn't do a thing," said Rolando. "We were standing right here the whole time, and we saw everything."

No doubt this teacher would have liked nothing better than to report me as a violent criminal. But Tito and Rolando's father was a Party member, and that gave them a certain status in his eyes.

"Well, he'd better not!" the man shouted. "This worm must learn his place!"

He walked away then, and the ringleader got up, his mouth opening and closing like a choirboy as he tried to breathe. He and his gang retreated, and Luis helped me to my feet. My boys closed around me.

"Are you all right?"

"You didn't hit him, did you?"

"Is your nose broken?"

Rolando gave me a handkerchief. I pressed it to my face, trying to stop the flow of blood. My nose didn't feel broken, but I knew it was going to swell and ache for days.

"I'm fine," I said. Then I held out my hand. "Thanks, guys. You probably saved my life."

"Listen, Calcines," said Tito, shaking my hand. "We decided we're gonna help you when we can. But we can't get into trouble, either. We sent them a message, so they know they can't get away with too much when we're around. But we can't be around you all the time, either." He shook his head and looked sorrowful. "It's gonna be rough, buddy," he said. "But you're gonna have to deal with it somehow."

"I can deal with anything," I said. "God doesn't give us anything we can't handle."

Talk of God was just as forbidden as talk of dissent, and Tito and Rolando automatically looked around to see if any teachers had heard. But I didn't care. I could certainly put up with playground harassment until the day the telegram of freedom arrived.

My only hope now was that the telegram wouldn't take too long.

Our troubles really began one night a couple of weeks later. I lay in my bed in the living room trying to sleep, but lately that had been hard. There was just too much going on in my head. I thought about the possibility that we would be moving to America, the "Land of Freedom to the north." There would be chewing gum and ketchup, and all the food I could eat. Once again, I would know the pleasures of thumbing through a brand-new comic book, the delightful scents of ink and fresh newsprint filling my nostrils. I would have a bicycle. I would have new clothes, maybe. Papa would get a good job, and we would live in a nice house on a nice street. I would play baseball with American boys, and I would learn English. The Calcines clan would become American.

Which meant, I guessed, that I would stop being me, and become someone else—someone who looked like me, and who had my name, but there the resemblance would end. Eduardo Calcines of Glorytown would cease to exist. I would be Eddy Calcines, American kid. It was all too much to think about, and I tossed and turned under my sheet.

Sometime in the middle of the night, I heard the sound that we had all come to dread: a military truck, turning down San Carlos Street. This was not a new sound—we often heard trucks pass our house. Then I would pull the covers up over my head and stick my fingers in my ears, because I knew what would happen next. There would be shouting, crying, screaming, breaking glass. Once I heard the terrifying sound of gunfire, though I never found out what it was about. I prayed that the truck would pass us by and stop in front of someone else's house—someone I didn't like, such as La Natividad, the crazy woman.

But the truck didn't pass us by. It stopped right outside our house. The squeaking of the brakes was like the howling of a legion of demons, striking terror into my heart.

Soldiers jumped from the back of the truck; boots pounded on pavement. Their equipment jangled, and their weapons made eerie clicking sounds as they prepared them as if to fire. Some ran up to the front door and pounded on it, screaming for us to open up. Others ran to the back of the house to make sure no one escaped.

I sat up in my bed, saw a soldier out the living room window, and for one unforgettable moment our eyes met. He was short, with a neat mustache, and even in the dim night I could see the hatred pouring from his eyes. *This must be a mistake. This man doesn't know us. How can he hate us this way?* It was my first face-to-face confrontation with one of Fidel's fanatics. One look at this man sent fear coursing through every speck of me.

The officer in charge was yelling, "Worms! Traitors!" Mama came running to open the front door, wrapping herself in a bathrobe. The officer pushed past her, came over to my bed, leaned over, and stuck his face in mine.

"Where is the worthless Yankee sympathizer known as Rafael Calcines? Let me see his filthy face—*now!*" he screamed. Flecks of spittle landed on my face, and I could smell food on his breath. Unlike us, he had eaten well that night. So it was true—the Communists favored their own, at least their officers, even though they said we were all equal.

I heard Papa get up. He came out of his bedroom already dressed. Probably he had known they would come one night soon, and he didn't want to have these animals in our house a moment longer than necessary. Yet he hadn't said anything about this to us. Why not?

"Here I am," he said.

"You! In the truck!" said the officer. "And don't give me any trouble, or I'll cut you down right here in front of your two little pups!"

The other soldiers had all come in, too. They pointed their guns at Papa, ready to blow his head off if he made one false move. Esther and I started crying. Mama was doing her best to hold it together, but the tension got the better of her.

"Where are you taking my husband?" she shrieked. "Why are you doing this? What gives you the right?"

"None of your business," sneered the officer. "He's the property of the state now. You don't like our Revolution? Fine! You don't have to be part of it. Let's go!"

And with that, Papa was hustled out the door, put into the truck, and driven away. He barely had time to glance around and look at us, trying his best to smile. That was when I understood that this was a direct result of Papa's application for the exit visa. The government was retaliating against us for implying that the Revolution was less than perfect. Now I understood why Papa hadn't warned us ahead of time. There was no point in getting us worked up over the inevitable.

"Mama!" Esther screamed. "What's happening?"

But for once, Mama had no words of reassurance. She remained silent, her face the color of the sheets.

As soon as the truck had rumbled away, the whole neighborhood came out to see who had been unlucky this time. Abuelo and Abuela were the first on the scene, and they knelt to embrace us.

"Don't you worry," Abuela crooned. "Your papa is strong, and he is smart. He will be fine. Just don't worry."

"But where is he?" I cried. "Where is my papa? Where did they take him?"

The grownups all exchanged glances.

"He is going to do some work for the government," Abuelo offered finally. "When his work is finished, then they will let him go. So don't worry, my little baseball player. Everything will be all right."

I could tell Abuelo didn't believe what he was saying, because he wouldn't look me in the eyes. But I also knew that there was nothing to be done. Abuela and Abuelo went back across the street to their house. I climbed into bed with Mama and Esther and lay staring at the ceiling, kicking my legs under the blanket.

"Eduar, stop that," Mama said.

"I can't sleep!" I said.

"Neither can I," Esther said. "I'm worried about Papa."

"Me, too," I said. "I already miss him. Where did they take him, Mama?"

"They took him—"

Mama stopped, choking up. She hated to let us kids see her upset. It was a mother's duty to remain strong and unshakable in front of her children, and the worse the times, the more serious that duty. But her husband had just been yanked out of bed in the middle of the night by jackbooted thugs with automatic weapons. The sanctity of our home had been shattered, our protector kidnapped. How was a woman expected to act as though nothing were wrong?

"They took him to a special camp," she finally said.

"Papa is going *camping*?" Esther said. She sounded unconvinced.

"Not exactly," Mama said, sniffling. "The government needs his help. They've taken him to a place where he can do work for them. Important work. Only Papa can do it. They wanted him specially, and they needed him right away."

"Then why was that man yelling at us and calling us names?"

"Oh, he was probably just in a bad mood," Mama said. "Maybe his wife burned his dinner."

"Maybe he stepped on a nail," Esther suggested.

"Maybe he fell into an outhouse," I said.

"That's probably just what happened," Mama said. "Now let's all try to get some sleep."

So I lay there and kept staring up at the ceiling, trying not to kick my legs, imagining Papa on a camping trip with lots of men with machine guns. I hoped he was having a good time, but somehow I doubted it. I was already as cynical and worldly-wise as someone twice my age. I knew full well that Papa wasn't on any camping trip, and I knew that the officer hadn't simply been in a bad mood. The government was coming after us now, and we were at their mercy until they decided to let us leave.

Remember the Lord

That first day after Papa was taken, I woke up feeling as if I were on a long slide into a dark abyss. Suddenly nothing seemed real to me anymore. Now that the privacy and security of our home had been shattered, it was clear to me that our lives were nothing more than illusions. The walls and roof could not protect us, but more than that, the very idea of "home" was gone. Our identity as a family had been destroyed. But, not quite eleven, I couldn't put this feeling into words, so I was stuck with a feeling of all-consuming emptiness. It was worse than hunger, worse than sadness, worse than fear. It was the feeling that there was nothing good left in the world.

I did what I always did when I felt low—I went across the street to my grandparents' house and climbed up the avocado tree onto the roof. The birds were singing as though everything was fine. I had come to love the sound of birds for that very reason—because they always seemed so close to me, and yet so distant from the problems of the world. I longed to fly away like them. Since that was impossible, I became proficient at bird calls.

I could, and often did, have long conversations with any winged friend that stopped by to roost in one of the fruit trees. I would think about all the things that were bothering me as I whistled, screeched, and clucked. I believed that the birds really understood what I was saying, and that their responses to me were words of comfort: *Don't worry! Everything up here is fine! Just fly away like us!* How I wished that I could.

Wild parakeets and parrots abounded in Cuba, and I had become adept at mimicking them. Another frequent visitor was the *mariposa*, which means butterfly, but is also the nickname given to the painted bunting, a colorful relative of the cardinal. Mockingbirds, doves, and hummingbirds were common. My old friend Pichilingo was still around, too. He was getting up there in rooster years, but his comb still stood upright and flaming red, and he still scratched and crowed and strutted around manfully in front of his few remaining hens.

Abuelo Julian came out into the yard. Normally he would have warned me not to break any of the roof tiles. But this morning he said nothing of the sort. I knew he was trying to be respectful of my feelings. This made me feel even worse. I wanted so much for things to go back to normal.

Instead Abuelo just stood there, sipping from a little cup of coffee. When he finished it, he looked up at me and tried to smile.

"You're getting so good at those bird calls, I couldn't tell at first if it was you or a parrot," he said. "If I hadn't heard you climb up the avocado tree, I wouldn't have known you were here."

I said nothing.

"You want to play catch?" he offered. "You have some time before school."

"No, thanks," I mumbled.

"You're worried about your papa."

I nodded. Tears threatened to wash down my cheeks. I tried Mama's trick of opening my eyes wide and looking up, but it didn't work.

"Come on down, niño. Let's talk."

Abuelo and I sat under the avocado tree. Abuela came out with a fresh cup of coffee. She seemed about to say something, but then, seeing that we needed to have a man-to-man talk, she went back inside. I'd managed to stop my tears, but I still sniffled. Abuelo rubbed my head with his strong and capable hand.

"Your papa," Abuelo said, "is a very brave man."

I nodded.

"He knew this would happen, and yet he went ahead with his decision anyway," Abuelo went on. "That takes a lot of courage."

"I know. But, Abuelo, where did he go?"

"What did your mama tell you?"

I snorted. "She gave us some line about how he went camping. But that was for Esther. I don't believe it."

Abuelo nodded. "Maybe you're old enough to be told these things," he said. "I never thought that shielding children from the truth of the world was a good idea. Better they should know what's really going on, because they have to deal with it anyway. Niño, your father has been taken to a prison work camp."

"He's in prison?" This was my worst fear come true. I nearly started to cry again.

But Abuelo said, "No, not prison, really. He's lost his freedom, but he's not in a jail cell. They've taken him out to the country, not far from my sugar mill. He's going to be working in the cane fields. This is what they call 'agricultural reform.' They'll work him hard, and they won't be polite about it. But I know Felo, and he will survive. And he'll get the chance to come home one weekend a month, to see you, Esther, and your mama."

At that, I brightened. This was a minor improvement over being in jail. We had gone to see Tío William a couple of times since he had been in jail, and it had been a terrible experience. The visiting room was a filthy concrete hole, with creeping green mildew on the walls and the scent of urine in the air. It was obvious that Tío and the other men were trying hard to hide how miserable they really were. But if Papa was allowed home every once in a while, it wouldn't be so bad.

"What about his hernia?" I asked. Papa had hurt himself a couple of years ago, and he wasn't supposed to do any heavy lifting or other hard labor until it got fixed.

Abuelo waved this off. "Listen, niño," he said, "God doesn't give us anything we can't handle. But if things ever get to be too much . . . He takes us up to heaven, where we live surrounded by His love and glory forever. There is nothing to fear, my boy. Nothing at all."

I guess Abuelo could see I wasn't convinced, because he said, "Come inside with me for a moment. I want to remind you of something."

In the house, we stood before Abuela's picture of Jesus, which, in defiance of all the laws of the state, still hung on the wall.

"This man, who was the Son of God," Abuelo said, "bore the most terrible punishments that any human could endure. And He did it for us, to show us how powerful His love was. Your papa knows Jesus, and he knows His power. Whenever his life feels too hard, he knows that all he has to do is pray, and God will take over. The Lord will never abandon your papa, and He will never abandon you, either, niño. You must never, ever forget that as long as you live. Promise?"

I nodded.

"I want to hear you say it," Abuelo said.

"Yes, Abuelito. I promise I will never forget about Jesus."

"Good boy. Now, it's time for school. Are you ready?"

"You mean, did I do my homework?"

"No. That is not what I mean."

I knew Abuelo wasn't talking about my homework, and he knew I knew. He was talking about the things that happened to me at school. They also happened between adults on the street.

"Yes, I'm ready," I said.

"What are you going to do when the teasing starts today?"

"What I've been doing since school started. Ignore it. Run away. Don't fight back."

Abuelo nodded. "It is a hard pill to swallow, niño. But you must remember that your papa is making a huge sacrifice for you. And if you get into trouble, the authorities can take away your visa forever. That means the army for you, and it means your family will be stuck here. So control your temper, and don't let them get to you. Remember the Lord, niño. He can help you, too."

"I will, Abuelo."

"Then you'd better get going. You don't want to be late and give them one more reason to get you in trouble."

School had ended up being no worse than usual that day—trouble didn't come until after school. As usual, my mother had come to get

Esther at noon, but my friends, for various reasons, weren't there to walk home with me.

I stood on the corner of a busy street, waiting for traffic to pass. Suddenly, a kid I didn't even know came up behind me and smacked me on the back of the head. I turned around and put my fists up. Then I remembered—no fighting.

"What the hell do you want?" I said. He was a few years older than I was, with a dirty face and patched-up clothes. He stood with his hands on his hips, a chilling smile on his face.

"You're Calcines, aren't you?"

"What of it?"

"Well, nothing, except I hear your mother is a prostitute," he said.

I could hardly believe my ears. "*What* did you say?" I roared.

"You heard me. Everyone in the neighborhood knows. Now that your father is a guest of the state, your mother needs to find some other way to support her little brats. Your sister's name is Esther, isn't it?"

"Leave my sister out of it. She's just a little girl."

"Who cares? A worm is a worm. Your mother probably is teaching her all the tricks of the trade. I hear that kind of thing runs in the family. What do you think your mother's been doing while you've been in school all day? Men have been coming and going through the front door like it was a train station. I would have gone myself, but I didn't have the five cents."

"You piece of dog crap, I'm gonna kill you," I growled.

"What? What did you say? Help! Police! A violent dissenter is making threats against me!"

I turned and ran across the street, not caring if I got hit by a car. As it happened, there was no traffic at the moment. But my new tormentor followed me, trailed now by a small crowd of curious onlookers—both children and adults—who were laughing and encouraging him.

"Your mother is a whore!" he screamed.

I ran faster now, so angry I thought I was going to go off like a nuclear bomb. In that moment, if I'd exploded, I would have leveled the whole city.

I was smaller than this kid, but like everyone else he was probably tired and hungry, so I easily outran him. I could still hear his shouts as I made it to San Carlos Street and my own home turf.

What scared me most was that he seemed to know all about me. How had he known my sister's name? How had he known my father was at a work camp? Who had told him these things?

"The government publishes the names of dissenters," Abuelo told me when I related what had happened. "That's how he knows. They print names, ages, even addresses."

"But why?" I shouted. My grandparents sat and listened, Abuela's hands wrestling each other in her lap, Abuelo sipping a little cup of coffee. "If they hate us so much, why don't they just let us leave tomorrow? It's cruel! They're doing it for fun!"

Abuelo nodded. "That's right," he said. "They are doing it for fun."

"But what kind of people would do such a thing?" I raged. "Who would say these things about Mama? Abuelo, I've never been so mad in all my life!"

"Eduar, one of the hardest lessons in life is that there are evil people in this world who take pleasure in hurting others," Abuela said. "They have no sense of right and wrong, and they don't care about your feelings. They are so unhappy and so far from decency that the only time they feel good is when they make others feel as bad as they do."

"I can't do this," I said. "I just can't. I felt like I couldn't even breathe. I'm—I'm—"

"Angry," observed Abuelo.

"Yeah," I said.

Their calmness and acceptance helped me to relax, and my shoulders slumped. My fists, which had been clenched all afternoon, became hands again.

"Abuelo, please help me. What should I do?" I asked.

Abuelo gave me a kind smile. Then he turned his eyes up to the wall, where the picture hung.

More Goodbyes

Right after Papa was taken away, the government finally did what we had been dreading. It closed Tío William's distribution company and confiscated everything: trucks, tanks, hoses, tools, and building. Tío had employed ten people, and he had hundreds of regular customers who depended on him for the gas to run their cars and the alcohol to fuel their stoves. We'd been allowed to keep the business running in his absence, but now those ten employees and their families, plus Abuelo Julian and Abuela Ana, who had also needed his help in spite of Abuelo's job, plus anyone who might have depended on Tío's drivers for black-market food, were out of luck. We realized we were about to join the masses of Cuban poor.

One day I walked in on my mother sitting alone in the kitchen, crying.

"Mama, what's the matter?" I asked.

Mama hated to be seen like this. She'd always despised the image of women as weaklings, and she never wanted her children to sense the despair that was taking over her heart. But she couldn't hide her tears, no matter how fast she dried them with her apron.

"I just feel so bad for poor William," she said. "He started out with a wagon that he pulled himself, because he couldn't even afford a horse! Twenty years later, he had a fleet of trucks with his name on them. He was an important man. And now these animals just step in and steal everything. Why?"

"Tío is tough," I said. "He'll figure something out."

"Aiee, Eduar, I know he will," said Mama. "I'm not worried about that. It's just . . . these are terrible times for Cuba. Terrible times. Everyone is being pushed to the limit, and some people can't handle it."

"You can handle it, can't you, Mama?" I asked, worried.

"Of course I can handle it," she snapped, straightening her back. "As long as I can draw breath into my lungs, I will survive, and so will you. So let's not have any talk about not handling it. Sometimes I wish things were the way they used to be, Eduar, that's all. But there's no use complaining about what you can't change. Remember that, niño."

"Yes, Mama," I said.

"But I do have to find a way to make some money," Mama said, sighing.

I knew that my many aunts and uncles had offered to do what they could, but Mama was too proud to accept handouts. Besides, everyone else was suffering just as much as we were.

"I can quit school," I told Mama. "I can find a way to make money."

"Are you crazy? The Communists would never allow it," she said. "Once they see you're gone, they'll come looking for you. And that's the kind of attention this family does not need."

"Well, if we don't get some money somehow, it won't matter what the Communists think, because we'll all be dead!" I said.

"Niño, you go to school, and let me worry about feeding us. I'm your mother. That's my job."

So I prayed that Mama would find a way to make enough money to keep on feeding us at least one meal a day.

Time passed slowly. Papa came home from his first month at the work camp on a weekend furlough. He looked sunburned and exhausted, and he was stooped with pain from his hernia. When he walked in the door, Esther and I were so happy that we cried, and once again Mama opened her eyes wide and looked up at the ceiling.

Mama had cautioned us against asking too many questions, but Esther and I were burning to know what life was like at the work camp.

"They work us like slaves," he said. "We spend fourteen or fifteen hours a day out in the fields. We get practically nothing for breakfast and only slightly more than that at lunch. At dinner, we get wormy hard bread and canned meat. Then we sleep like dead men until the sun comes up, when they wake us by screaming in our faces and pushing us out the door again."

"Felo, you don't have to talk about it," Mama said, her voice trembling.

"No, I want them to know."

"But they're only children!"

"The Communists don't care if they're only children," Papa said. "To them, we're just worms. So I want you to listen, kids. This is how the Communists treat people who dare to disagree with them. We sleep in an old chicken pen, and believe me when I say they didn't clean it out first. After all day in the fields, they herd us into a stall and hose us down with cold water."

Esther and I listened sadly. Our poor papa!

"And that's not all," Papa said. "Some men get beaten up by the guards for no reason. Or they are told cruel lies about what their wives are doing to survive back home. A lot of men can't take it. They used to be doctors, or lawyers, or businessmen like Tío William. Some have worked in offices all their lives. Their hands are soft, and their spirits are weak. But they had good minds. How do these Communists think they are going to create the perfect workers' paradise, when they're killing our best and brightest?" He shook his head.

"What happens to them?" I asked.

"Sometimes they go mad, and sometimes they just lie down and die," Papa said.

"Felo! That's too much!" Mama said. "You're going to terrify them!"

"And why shouldn't they be terrified?" Papa said. "It's not like we can hide from them what's happening. They may be only children, but they have eyes and ears, Concha. Don't you think I wish we lived in a world where little ones didn't have to deal with such things? Of course I do! But we don't, and there is nothing to be gained from pretending otherwise!"

Esther began to cry. "I don't want you to die, Papa!" she said.

"Papa's not going to die," I told her. "He's too tough. Right, Papa?"

"They're never going to get me down," he said. His voice was full of a bitter strength that I admired. "They'll try, but they won't break me. I can take anything they dish out."

Then I noticed a burlap bag that Papa had brought with him.

"What's in there?" I asked.

He opened it and removed a chunk of hard bread and some cans of meat.

"My rations," he said. "I tried to save as much as I could to share with my family. The guards didn't want to let me, but I told them it was my food and I could do with it what I wanted. I thought they were going to shoot me right then and there. But I didn't care. It's in God's hands when I die. I just couldn't stand the thought of my two little ones going hungry."

When Mama heard this, she put her hands over her mouth and opened her eyes wide yet again. "Give it to me, Felo. I'll make us something to eat," she said when she'd recovered her composure. "Are you hungry?"

"I just want to sleep," Papa said. "But first I want to hold my kids. Come here and sit on my lap, you two. Do you know how much I've missed you?"

Esther and I climbed carefully onto his lap.

"We pray for you every night," I told Papa.

"I pray for you, too," Papa said. "Which reminds me. Conchita, I hope you still aren't taking the kids to church."

"Church? No," Mama said. "Not after what happened to Aida."

"Good," he said quietly.

Tía Aida, the mother of my cousins Luis and Ernesto, had been served with papers that accused her of "false indoctrination" and "corrupting the morals of children"—her own children. Her crime was sending her boys to weekly religious education classes. If Tía Aida had been convicted, under the law she could have been sent to prison for ten years. The Jesuit superintendent in Cienfuegos had made a special plea to the authorities, and the charges had been dropped. But this incident scared Tía so badly that not only did she stop sending her boys to religious education, she never went to church again. And neither did we.

Christians were persecuted all over Cuba. Abuelo had told us a horrible story that he'd heard from a friend at the sugar mill. His friend had been on the street when he heard a strange chanting. Somewhere, people were yelling, "Long live Christ the King!" Daring to ask a passerby what was going on, he was told that the chanting was coming from a nearby prison. The people making all the noise had been arrested for saying that God was greater than Fidel.

"But what is going to happen to them?" he had asked.

"They're going to be shot in the morning," came the reply.

Abuelo's friend got away from there in a hurry.

Papa's visit was all too short. It was his responsibility to get back to the work camp on time, but the only method of travel was the bus, which was so unreliable that he had to leave well in advance.

"Why don't you just run away, Papa?" I suggested. "You can go hide in the country! They'll never find you!"

"Believe me, niño, not only would they find me, but they would take it out on Mama and you kids," he said. "You don't want to give them any reason at all to come down hard on us, or we'll never get out of here."

"You're right," I admitted. "We'd better not attract any attention to ourselves."

"That's my boy. Now you're learning how to think ahead, instead of just acting impulsively. Don't forget, it's only a matter of time before that telegram comes," Papa said.

I hadn't wanted to ask about the telegram, but now that he brought it up, I said, "Papa, how much longer do you think we'll have to wait?"

"That's in God's hands, too. I have no idea. But it's going to come in a jeep, delivered by an officer. He's going to be rude, but who cares? Because when it comes, exactly one week to the day later, we will be on an airplane to the United States of America. And then, my little ones . . ."

Papa grew speechless and misty-eyed.

Then he kissed each of us goodbye and got on the bus.

Señora Felicia had been serious when she told me she didn't ever want to hear another word from me. A few days after Papa left, I was sitting at my desk, trying not to get into trouble, when I realized I had to have a bowel movement. I raised my hand, but she ignored me. My waving became frantic, and I knew she had to know why, but this sadistic woman continued to ignore me until the inevitable happened: I lost control of my bowels, right there in my seat.

The smell permeated the air instantly. All my classmates began to gag and retch. Then they looked around to see who had done it. Their laughter rang throughout the room.

"Calcines!" screamed Señora Felicia. "Get out of my class!"

I got up and ran out of the room, holding my pants up until I got to the toilet. There I cleaned myself up as best I could, too humiliated even to cry. Instead of toilet paper, we had only pieces of scrap paper and pages from old magazines. But these were so harsh and thick that they just made the mess worse.

When I was done, I thought for sure I'd be allowed to go home, but there was a kid waiting for me in the hallway. He was pinching his nose shut with his fingers.

"What do you want?" I asked.

"Señora Felicia says you have to stay and line up for dismissal," he told me.

"You're kidding," I said. "What does she want from me?"

"How should I know? Just don't stand next to me!" he said.

I lined up with everyone else, trying to ignore the taunts and jibes of the children within smelling range. When the bell rang, I ran faster than I ever had before. At home, I washed my clothes before Mama could find them. I didn't want any more people than necessary to know.

But the damage had been done. Word got around, and soon it was open season on Eduardo Calcines. In addition to being a worm, I was a poopypants. Even Rolando, Tito, and Luis took their jibes at me for a few days.

"It's that damn Señora Felicia!" I told them. "She knew I had to crap and she just ignored me!"

They knew it was true, but they laughed nonetheless.

One day soon after, Abuela came charging into our house, her eyes bright with excitement.

"What is it?" Mama asked.

"It's Arturo and Dinorah," Abuela replied. "They've gotten their telegram!"

"What!" I shouted. "When?"

"Just today! An hour ago!"

I ran to the door and looked up and down the street. We had applied for our visas around the same time, and this news gave me hope that our telegram would be coming, too. But San Carlos Street was empty, except for a dog sitting in the middle of the road, licking himself. I went back inside, discouraged.

"It's not fair!" I groused. "We've been waiting just as long as they have!"

"Eduardo Francisco Calcines!" said Mama sharply. "We should be happy, not resentful. Your aunt and uncle and little cousin are going to be together with Arturito again, and they're going to be free. When you see them, I want you to offer them your congratulations. And if I hear one word of jealousy from you, your bottom will feel my hairbrush. M'entiendes?"

"Yes, Mama," I said.

"Don't forget, niño, it's a lottery," Abuela said. "You never know who is going to get picked. It could just as easily have been you. Your time is coming."

Tío Arturo and Tía Dinorah's son, Arturito, had gone to America in 1962, through the Peter Pan Program. There had been rumors that Cuban children would be taken away from their families and put in indoctrination camps run by the Cuban government. The Catholic Church, working with the United States government, was able to find temporary homes for some boys and girls with Catholic families in America. It had been hard for all of us to see Arturito go, but especially Tío Arturo and Tía Dinorah. It was wonderful news that they would all be together again.

My aunt and uncle had just a week to get ready. They couldn't pack much because of the law that said almost everything in their house was considered the property of the state. On the day they were leaving, the army sent an officer with a list of their possessions, so he could make sure they weren't going to "steal" anything. Never mind that all those things had been paid for with their own money before the Revolution—if so much as one square foot of carpet or one piece of silverware was missing, the officer threatened, their visas would be revoked.

The entire extended family had come to say goodbye, and we all held our breath as this self-important little martinet went through the house, checking off item after item and asking questions in a shrill tone. But finally he left, satisfied, and we breathed a sigh of relief.

Then the sad part came.

Abuela was suffering more than anyone. First she hugged her granddaughter Cary goodbye. Then she turned to Dinorah. Abuela had been uncharacteristically quiet all week. I could feel the sadness coming off her in waves. I'd hugged her as often as possible, just so she wouldn't feel so bad. But it hadn't helped. It made me realize that no matter how old a woman is, the bond with her children is the strongest bond there is, and nothing makes the breaking of it easier.

Abuela and Tía Dinorah stepped off to the side now, clasping each other close, not speaking a word. Only then did Abuela give in to her feelings and cry. We all remained silent. Tío Arturo finally had to remind his wife gently that they absolutely could not afford to be late for the plane, because they wouldn't get a second chance.

"Goodbye, Mama," said Dinorah. "I—I can't—I don't know what to—"

Abuela nodded, letting her know that she didn't need to go on.

Even I could see that it wasn't possible to put such feelings into words.

"I love you, Dinorah," Abuela said.

Abuelo couldn't speak at all. He hugged his daughter and Cary, and shook Tío Arturo's hand.

"*Hasta luego*, Papa," said Dinorah. See you later. Abuelo nodded in agreement. Dinorah was refusing to say goodbye. Instead she held out hope that they would meet again, soon.

Then we all crowded around as they got into the taxi, reaching out to touch them one last time. Most of the people there that day knew they probably would never see Arturo, Dinorah, and Cary again. If I did see them again, I realized, it would be in America, in a future that I couldn't even imagine.

As we watched the taxi go down the street and turn the corner, Abuelo put his arm around Abuela and held her as she sobbed. Then he led her into the house, where she stayed for the rest of the day, allowing no visitors at all—not even me.

It seemed that everyone else was getting their telegrams before we did. Two other families in our extended clan—the Acostas and the Garcías—had also applied for visas. The Garcías' telegram came, and this farewell scene was repeated. Other families of dissenters I knew from school had gotten their telegrams, too. It was maddening.

"The government is doing it on purpose," I told my mother. "They hate us more than anyone else."

"Nonsense," Mama said. "That's not true. They hate us all equally."

"Well then why is it taking so long?"

"Niño, no more complaining," Mama told me. "Complaining is a sign of weakness, and with your father gone, you are the man of the house. We have no room for wimps here."

"I wish I could be a wimp just for an hour a day," I said. "It's hard being the man of the house all the time!"

Mama said, "You think I don't know about hard? Someday I'll tell you how hard all this has been for me. But now is not the time for that. We all have burdens in life, niño, and it makes me very sad to see my young son have to shoulder such a big one. But you must do it without complaining, because that's what your father would do if he were here. Pretend he's standing next to you, watching everything you do. Maybe that will make it a little easier."

I was too old for such little-kid games, but all the same, Mama's advice worked. I pretended that Papa and I were having long conversations, and even though they were imaginary, I always felt better afterward. As I sat on my grandparents' roof, surrounded by my bird friends, I imagined what Papa would say, recalling the sound of his deep voice and the feel of his warm hand on the back of my neck.

"Be a man, son!" I would say to myself, imitating his way of talking. "Don't let the family down! You can do it!"

Then I would feel a little bit better . . . but only a little.

Panetelas de Vainilla

One afternoon a few weeks after Papa's first visit home, Mama called us into the kitchen and sat us down.

"Guess what? I am going to make *panetelas de vainilla*," she said.

"Yum!" Esther and I said. Panetelas de vainilla were vanilla sugar cakes, simple concoctions of sugar, butter, flour, and vanilla. In better times, they were a favorite treat. Now the ingredients were almost impossible to come by. It had been ages since we'd tasted Mama's panetelas.

But Mama said, "No, no. They are not for you."

"Who are they for, then?" I asked.

"They're for sale, my niños. I am going to sell them on the black market."

"But, Mama!" I said. "If you get caught, you'll be reported! You might even get sent to jail!"

"I have no choice, Eduar," Mama said. "I'm telling you this because I am going to need your help. Esther, you will help me make them, and Eduar, you will deliver the panetelas to your tía Luisa. I've spoken to her, and she's agreed to sell them for me. And you will both keep quiet about it. You must not talk about it with anyone, not even your grandparents."

"Aren't you going to tell them?"

"Of course I'll tell them. That's not the point. You have to learn, kids, that in these times, it's better not to speak of anything that puts us at risk, even with the people you trust. If you don't talk about it, then no one can overhear you. You understand?"

"Yes, Mama," we both said.

"Good," she said.

Mama's first task was to locate the ingredients for the panetelas. The only thing that wasn't in short supply in Cuba was sugar. But one lady had extra butter for sale, another had a few cups of flour, yet another had the vanilla. None of these things was available in stores anymore, except to people with strong political connections. They had all been obtained illegally, and Mama had to barter for them in secret. She had to swear her suppliers to secrecy, too. That was no problem—they would have been in just as much trouble as we were.

Once Mama got her ingredients, she set to work making the panetelas. Then I was given the job of transporting them to Tía Luisa's house. Tía Luisa was my father's sister. She was married to Tío Jesús and they had a daughter, Maricela. They lived pretty far away, by the port.

One day, as I came out of our house with a bag full of panetelas, I saw that my friends were hanging around in front of the Jagua Movie House on the corner.

"Calcines!" Rolando called. "Where are you going? Let us come with you!"

"No!" I said, walking faster. "I have to go alone."

"Come on," said Tito. "We're bored, and Luis is sick again." My cousin had terrible asthma attacks and was often sick.

"What's in that bag?" Tito asked.

"None of your business," I said. "You guys are worse than the C.D.R. Now leave me alone!"

"Fine," said Tito, obviously hurt. "You want to go by yourself, you go ahead. See what happens to you if some gang catches you. They'll break your legs!"

"They'll have to do worse than that to get this bag from me."

"Why? What's in it?"

"Nice try," I said. "See you later."

I had to choose how to travel: by bus or on foot. As Abuelo had explained to me, all the auto parts in Cuba had been "nationalized," meaning they'd been stolen by the army and the police for use in their own vehicles. Their Soviet-made replacements were of such poor quality that they often either broke on first use, or they didn't work to begin with. The chance that the bus was running at all was only about fifty-fifty. If it did come, it would probably be so full that not even a little kid could cram in. And the bus was slower than a lame snail. In the time it took me to ride to the port, I could have walked there and back. So I chose to go on foot.

The port held a lot of pleasant memories for me. When I was younger, Abuelo Julian and I used to go there sometimes, to meet up with his friends from the sugar mill. They'd started working there together just after the turn of the century, when they were still in their late teens or early twenties. One of their favorite pastimes was to sit on shady benches in the cool of the morning, sipping coffee, smoking cigars the size of zeppelins, and reveling in the cool ocean breeze.

I loved going to visit these old men. They all smelled like Abuelo, with aftershave on their cheeks and scented water in their hair. Whenever a lady walked by, they lifted their hats and nodded. And they were full of stories of their youth: who could work the most hours in a row, who was the strongest and the fastest and the best. They joshed each other in a constant, pattering stream, and I, young sponge that I was, took in every word.

Once I asked Abuelo why we didn't go to meet his friends anymore.

"You know, Fidel has outlawed public gatherings," he replied.

It was against the law for my grandfather to sit and talk with his friends. Yet another wonderful Cuban tradition was now nothing more than a memory.

Another reason I loved the port was visiting Tía Luisa, Tío Jesús, and my cousin Maricela. Tía Luisa was short and plump, with fair hair that she wore on top of her head, and with beautiful green eyes, just like all the Calcineses. She was perhaps the friendliest and warmest person I knew. She maintained a permanent open-door policy. Anyone was welcome in her kitchen, day or night, and whether she knew you or not, she greeted you with a big hug. If you were hungry, she fed you—and, because Tía traded clandestinely with sailors from all over the world, she always had something tasty in her kitchen. If you had no place to go, she would even put you up. Once, for a while, an old Chinese man had lived with them. Nobody knew how he had come to be in Cuba. One day he just showed up, and a few weeks later he was gone again.

On this particular day, I made it to Tía's without any trouble.

"Eduar!" she greeted me. As usual, she was in her housedress and slippers and she was kneading some dough on the table. A smear of flour decorated her forehead, and a broad smile lit her face. "How's it going?"

"*Hola*, Tía," I said.

"How many did you bring me today?"

"A dozen."

"Put them there." With a nod, she indicated a spot on the counter. "Now, pick up that envelope. It's got your mama's money in it. Tell her I can sell all she can make. The sailors love them, especially the Russians."

"I can't carry any more than this," I said. "I need to be able to move fast if I have to."

"Have you had any trouble?"

"Nothing I can't handle. Where's Maricela today?"

"She's over at a neighbor's house, playing with a friend. How are your friends treating you these days?"

"Who?" I asked.

"Your friends—those Caballero brothers—their father is a Communist, isn't he?"

I nodded. "He joined the Party a few years ago."

"And still they hang out with you?"

"He didn't say they couldn't. We've been friends since we were babies. We don't talk about stuff like politics, anyway."

"All the same, you be careful what you say around them. They might let something slip to their father without meaning to. Then we'll all be in trouble."

"I know how to keep my mouth shut, Tía, and besides Luis, those guys are my best friends," I said. "In fact, I think—well, can you keep a secret?"

Tía threw her head back and laughed. "Can I keep a secret? Who do you think you're talking to? The black-market queen of Cienfuegos, that's who! Go ahead, tell me. I'm so full of secrets already I won't even notice one more."

"The way they talk about America I have a feeling they'd like to leave Cuba, too."

"Really? The sons of Communists? How surprising."

"They don't have it any better than we do. And just because their dad is a Communist doesn't mean they are, too," I said.

"Good for them. Shows they're smart."

"Yeah, well, I don't hang around with dummies."

Tía smiled. "Eduardo, have a bite to eat, and then you'd better get on your way."

"*Gracias*, Tía."

Leaving Tía's, I had a bunch of cash—about twenty pesos, equal then to six or seven American dollars—and I stashed most of it in my underwear. All I could think about was all the wonderful food this money would buy, and how desperate things would get if I lost it. I was so nervous about getting stopped by the police that I felt sure my pants were transparent.

My next stop was the home of Tío Amado, my father's older brother. He lived in the barrio of Tulipan, and it so happened that next door to his house was a market. Tío had long ago made a point of becoming friends with the man who ran it. Thanks to this connection, we were sometimes able to purchase a ration of real meat. It was still pathetically inadequate—one pound per person, per month—but it was better than nothing, and sometimes the shopkeeper would throw in a few extra scraps. If there was no meat available, then I would at least be able to buy a few loaves of fresh bread from Tío's friend, instead of the stale bricks that we got at our usual store. So off to Tío Amado's I went.

Tío took me next door to the market, but there was no meat left, so I bought four big loaves of bread and said goodbye to my uncle. Now I had to decide again—walk home, or take the bus? It was hot by now, so I decided I would ride. I would have to wait at least an hour at the bus stop, but I needed a break, so I sat down on the curb. Papa was coming home this weekend, and Abuela would take some of this bread and make bread pudding to celebrate, and then we would sit up late and tell stories . . .

Ping! A pebble bounced off my forehead.

I shot to my feet and looked around. There was no one in sight.

"Who threw that?" I yelled. "Coward! Show yourself!"

Ping! Another rock, a bigger one, hit me on the temple. This one broke the skin, and blood began to trickle down my cheek.

Suddenly, I couldn't stand it anymore. "That's it!" I said. "You're a bunch of little girls! Get out here right now, and I'll break every bone in your bodies!"

From around the corner appeared a gang of boys—four or five of them. Their leader was the biggest kid my age I'd ever seen. His knuckles practically dragged on the cement.

"What did you say?" the big one said. "Who are you talking to?"

"You!" I said. "I'm going to wipe the street with your face. Let's go, right now."

"I'm ready whenever you are, punk," said this behemoth.

Then I remembered the bread. Looking down at the bags at my feet, I realized that if I lost this fight, the bread would be lost, too. These kids looked like they were even hungrier than I was. The leader of the gang caught on right away.

"What's in those bags?" he demanded. "Is it food?"

"None of your business!" I said.

Quickly, I sized up my options. There weren't many. I could defeat this kid in a fight, but there was no way I could defend the bread from the others at the same time.

I wasted no more time. I dashed back across the street to Tío's—just as he opened the door.

"Booooooooy!" he bellowed. *"What is going on out here?"*

I tossed the bread into his house.

"Tío, watch that bread for me!" I said.

"What do those kids want?" he demanded.

"They want to fight!"

"Well? What are you waiting for? Get over there and kick their butts!"

"Tío, I'm working on it! I just need to make sure the bread is safe!"

"Bread, shmead! There has not been a Calcines yet who's backed down from a fight! Get in there and mix it up, boy!"

"Aaaaaaaaaagh!" I yelled, turning and putting on my best game face.

The effect of Tío's presence was visible on the faces of the gang. Now they didn't look so brave, and the big one didn't even look so big anymore. But there were still four or five of them, and only one of me. I had to adopt a new strategy. Quickly I decided on a technique that I'd been practicing in private—the Helicopter of Death.

The basic theory behind the Helicopter of Death was that I would swing both my fists as wildly and quickly as possible. Come to think of it, it was a technique similar to the one Tío William had used during the rumble of Noche Buena. My hope was that I would score enough random hits to convince the enemy to retreat. When the odds were this bad, it was the only tactic that made any sense.

I charged at the gang, eyes closed, screaming.

But I connected with nothing. I opened my eyes, and all I could see was dust. And all I could hear was Tío Amado's laughter. I turned to see him doubled over in the doorway, slapping his knees.

"What was that? Boy, I'm telling you, that was the best fighting I've ever seen! Hooah! Yah! I now know that you are a Calcines, niño! Wait'll I tell your father! Hee hee hee!"

He wheezed and puffed a few minutes longer, and then he paid me the ultimate compliment: "I'm proud of you, *sobrino*! Now, nephew, take your bread and get on home before your mother starts to worry!"

I needed no further urging. I grabbed the bread, decided that the bus was a lost cause, and started walking.

When Papa came home the next weekend, as promised, Tío Amado told him all about what had happened. Afterward, Papa came to me and put a hand on my shoulder.

"I hear you defended yourself very bravely, my boy," he said.

"I tried, Papa," I said.

"You tried, and you succeeded," he said. "I'm not happy to hear that you were fighting, but I'm proud that you didn't back down, even when the odds were against you." He was silent for a moment, his eyes twinkling. Then he said, "I've been thinking about something. What would you say to a little reward?"

"A reward?" What could it be? "Sure, Papa! That would be great! What is it?"

"There's this man I know who raises tropical fish in his home. I think Mama and Esther would like to have a fish around the house, don't you? Maybe you and I should go over there and see what he has for sale." Papa winked at me. "You know, I hear that man has a very pretty daughter about your age, too. Maybe you'll make a new friend."

I blushed. "You think?"

"What do you say? Let's go."

"Right now?"

"Yes, right now!"

I knew how tired Papa must have been, and how uncomfortable his hernia was making him. But that he wanted to spend time with me proved to me all over again what I already knew—I had the most loving father in the world. And it was an honor to stand next to him at the bus stop, feeling his warm hand on the back of my neck, and listening to his deep voice, knowing for a change that I didn't have to imagine his presence, because he was right there with me.

The Ashes of Spring

One morning early in 1967, I awoke to find San Carlos Street covered in a light coating of ash. This was a yearly occurrence, and I knew what it meant: the sugarcane harvest had ended. Abuelo had explained to me that after cutting the cane, the workers set fire to the fields to clear the stubble. All over Cuba, the same thing was happening. For several days, the air above our island grew as dark as if a volcano had erupted.

I went into Abuela Ana and Abuelo Julian's yard and held out my hands. Flakes of burnt cane collected on my palms. I looked at them glumly. The ashes of spring always gave me a pit in my stomach, because they meant that Abuelo would be going away soon.

At that moment, Abuelo himself came out onto his porch, holding a little cup of coffee. "In the north in America," he said, "snow falls all winter, just like this. The children go sledding and skiing on it. Someday you will, too."

"I'm not even sure I want to go to America anymore," I told him. "Maybe we should just stay here. Then they would let Papa out of the work camp, and there wouldn't be any more of this waiting."

"And you can forget about your dreams of freedom, too, in that case." Abuelo looked at me with concern. "What's the matter, niño? You look sad."

"You know what's the matter!"

"Aha. You're upset because I'm going away again."

I nodded. When the harvest ended, the refining process began. This was where Abuelo's expertise came in. As First Sugar Master, his presence was required for every moment of the three to four months it took to render tons and tons of cane into sugar. It meant that he had to live at the mill, twenty miles away. When Abuelo left, I had no one to play catch or talk about life with. And with Papa gone, I was without my two most important male role models. It was going to be a lonely spring.

"Don't be sad," Abuelo told me. "You're practically a man now. You have two households to be in charge of while I am gone—yours and mine. And make sure the women listen to you in my absence!"

"Yeah, right," I said. "They burn my butt if I so much as talk back to them!"

"Even so, you must behave like a man," Abuelo said. "Life gives us challenges, niño, but the Lord helps us handle them. For every problem, there is a way to deal with it. Just remember that."

"Well, then, what's the way to deal with the Communists?"

"Don't worry about the Communists. Just worry about your family. God will help us find a way through these times. And he expects us to continue doing our best, not to sit around and complain. That's why I'm going to the mill again this year, niño, and that's why you must not walk around with this long face. Esther looks up to you. Your job is to give her encouragement, and to make your mama's and abuela's lives easier by being helpful and staying out of trouble. M'entiendes?"

"Yes, Abuelo," I said. "But don't you think you're getting a little old to work so hard? Maybe it's time to let someone younger take over."

Abuelo stiffened. For a moment, I thought he was going to get angry. But then he relaxed and smiled.

"Listen, niño," he said. "It took me a long time to work my way up from a simple field hand to the most trusted and important position in the mill, and I can tell you right now that I will not stop working until the day I drop dead. None of these young men knows as much as I do about sugar. They need me. If they didn't, they wouldn't ask me to come, would they? These Communists may be running the show now, but you can't make sugar with propaganda!"

"Why are you going to help them, if they're not forcing you to?" I asked.

"I'm not going to the mill for the sake of the Communists," he said. "I'm going because Cuba is sugar. It's been an important part of Cuban life for a very long time, and it will continue to be long after this idiotic Revolution is nothing more than an unpleasant memory. Besides, to make sugar, you need experience and know-how, and these stupid Communists possess neither."

"Well, why can't you just teach them what you know, so you can stay home from now on?"

"Because I like to work and it takes years to learn all that I know," Abuelo replied. "You think I can just give them a few pointers? To master the art of sugaring requires a lifetime of patience. And patience, it seems to me, is something you could use a little more of, my boy. You're acting like a caged animal these days."

"I can't help it!" I told him. "Everything is up in the air, and I don't know what's what anymore. Waiting for this telegram is driving me crazy."

"Don't worry about the telegram," Abuelo said. He looked away, probably so I couldn't see his eyes welling up with tears. "It will come when it comes. There's nothing to be done about it, so you might as well just think about something else."

I, too, grew misty-eyed. To hide my emotions, I asked, "Can I have a little of your pomade?"

Abuelo took me into the house and put some pomade in my hair. Then he combed it back.

"Slick as a groom on his wedding day," he said. Then he dabbed aftershave on my cheeks. "What a handsome boy," he said. "Let's see that wink you've been practicing."

I had a lazy left eyelid, which had never bothered me until I realized it meant I couldn't wink. Girls always fell for guys who winked at them, at least if the movies were to be believed. I'd been practicing in the mirror for weeks. Finally, I'd gotten that stupid eyelid to move on its own. I showed Abuelo now, and he laughed and clapped his hands.

"Excellent!" he said. "That worthless doctor told us you might lose that eye completely. And now look! You're a regular Don Juan!"

"Did you have a lot of girlfriends when you were young, Abuelo?" I asked.

"Niño, I have been in love with only one woman my entire life, and the day I married her was the best day of all!" Abuelo said, very loudly. Then he bent down and whispered in my ear, "But let me tell you, when I wed your grandmother, there were a lot of brokenhearted girls in Rodas!"

"I heard that!" Abuela yelled from the living room.

"Heard what? I didn't say anything!" Abuelo said. Then he elbowed me in the side, one hand over his mouth.

The next day, the hated brown company car showed up to take Abuelo away. The whole family gathered in the front yard to say good-bye and wish him a safe and successful trip.

That spring, Tío William was released from prison and we thought it was a miracle that the government released him when they were supposed to. It had been a long and trying ordeal for him. He had been a massive man; now we could count his bones through his skin and he kept more to himself, smiling rarely and never laughing.

I had a hard time understanding this change in him. On one of his visits home Papa explained: "The Communists were very cruel to your uncle. He had spoken out to the guards when someone's rights were being trampled, and spoke for all prisoners when they had a demand. This earned him the respect of the other prisoners—and the constant torment of the guards. They barely fed him and sometimes they kept him for weeks in a cell that was so tiny he could neither lie down nor stand up. There were rats and bugs. He could feel them crawling over him at night. Whenever he fell asleep, the guards would pour cold water over him to wake him up."

"But why would they do that?" I asked.

"Torture," Papa replied. "They were going to break his spirit."

"What else did they do to him?"

"You are too young to hear such things, niño."

Years later, I learned the worst of what had happened to Tío. One day, the guards took him and several other men out to a field and made them dig a large pit. This, they were told, would be their grave.

When the men had finished digging, the guards lined them up in front of the hole and told them they were about to die. Then they raised their weapons and fired blanks.

The guards thought it was a big joke. It wasn't funny to the prisoners. One of them was so traumatized that he went mad and had to be committed to a mental institution.

Tío regained some of his strength and personality. But the trials he underwent in prison, coupled with the loss of his daughter, altered him forever. Instead of the great, happy bear of a man everyone knew and loved, he became a quiet, brooding presence in the background. But he wasn't completely broken. We could still count on him for a smile or a little joke when the situation called for it, and the entrepreneurial spirit dies hard, even under such repressive regimes. Tío bought a new truck with the small amount of money we'd saved for him in his absence, before his business was closed. He began to operate a cartage service, hauling trash and goods for people—sometimes even for the government. He told my father that this was his way of showing them who was better. He had decided to stay in Cuba and was determined to keep working until they stood him up against a wall and shot him, or until he dropped dead, whichever came first.

If I needed an example of how to behave in difficult times, I didn't have to look any further than my own family. One day, when I was hiding on the roof as usual, I heard voices raised in alarm. Climbing down quickly, I ran inside to see what was going on. My godmother, Magalys, was in the living room, wringing her hands.

"Your abuela has fallen outside the store and hurt herself," she told me. "Go tell your mama. I'm going to the hospital."

"What happened?" I asked.

"She tripped and fell. She has a nasty cut on her forehead," she said. "There was blood everywhere, and she's going to need stitches. But I think she's going to be fine."

I ran to get Mama and Esther, and we waited together for Magalys to come back with Abuela. When they finally showed up, it was nearly dark out. Abuela looked strange with a neat row of black sutures and a wicked-looking bruise on her forehead. Mama helped her to the rocking chair, and she sat down gingerly.

"I'm fine, I'm fine," she said in response to our anxious inquiries. "I don't know what happened. I was just stepping out of the door when I slipped on something, and the milk went everywhere. Magalys, was it all ruined?"

"It was, Abuela," said Magalys. "But don't worry about the milk. The important thing is that you're okay."

"What an old idiot I am!" Abuela said. "Who cares if I'm okay? The children needed that milk, and now they have none!"

"Don't worry about it," Mama soothed her. "We'll get more on the black market. It's okay."

"Curses on this stupid Revolution!" Abuela muttered. Then she looked up at the picture of Jesus on the wall and crossed herself. "Forgive me, Lord, for speaking that way," she said. "But why should the little ones have to suffer for the idiocy of adults? If someone has to go without, let it be me. The children have already seen too much."

Within the hour, the house filled with neighbors and family members. All of them had heard what happened, and they wanted to offer Abuela their best wishes for a speedy recovery. I think most of them were surprised to see her sitting up in the living room as though nothing had happened. They'd been expecting to find her in bed, but Abuela would rather have died than let everyone think she was a frail old woman.

It was just like my family to turn any event at all, even an unfortunate one, into a reason for socializing. Soon people seemed to forget why they were there, and they began laughing, joking, and generally having a good time. That was the best medicine there was for Abuela. She sat in her rocking chair, listening and smiling. Tío William came through the door about halfway through the evening. I perked up when I saw him.

"Mama!" he greeted Abuela cheerfully. "What have I told you about drinking rum during the daytime!"

"Oh, stop it, you bigheaded idiot," Abuela said. "You know I never touch the stuff!"

"And what have I told you about waiting in line? Why should you stand there for an hour and get so tired you trip, while any one of us can go get the milk for you? Next time, send Eduar!"

"Yeah, send me," I said without enthusiasm. Waiting in line was my least favorite activity in the world, though I would have done it for Abuela.

"William," said Abuela, "do you want something to eat?"

"Look at her! She's wounded, and she wants to cook something," Tío William said. "Mama, if you had any food in your kitchen, I would eat it. But you don't, so I won't."

"I'll check anyway," said Abuela, getting up.

"She doesn't listen in the slightest," Tío William said. He walked up behind her as she headed into the kitchen and slapped her on the butt. "Sit down!" he said. "Let someone else do the work for a change!"

"Leave me alone, little boy!" Abuela barked at him. I always thought it was hilarious when Abuela talked that way to Tío William, because he was so much bigger than she was. That he had come out of her body amazed me.

When Tío William left a few minutes later, I followed him out to the porch.

"Tío, can I have some money?" I asked.

He turned and scowled. "Who do I look like, Rockefeller? You're going to break me, sobrino!" But he reached into his pocket and pulled out a *diez centavos*—a coin worth about ten cents. "Here," he said. "Invest it wisely."

I held it up and looked at it, marveling at the kind of man Tío was. He'd lost his daughter, been sent to prison, lost his business, and still he could crack jokes and be generous. I admired him now more than ever.

"Do you have something to say to me?" Tío William growled.

"Thank you, Tío," I said.

"You're welcome," Tío William said, winking, and then he turned and went down the street to his own house.

La Natividad

By some miracle, I passed sixth grade and would be going to Nguyen Van Troy Middle School in the fall. I'd gotten a little taller, though not nearly enough to satisfy me, and I'd grown stronger as well. I'd become a fast runner, too—my clandestine trips to Tía Luisa's now took me only a couple of hours.

My grades hadn't shown a whit of improvement, but luckily Mama had bigger things to worry about. When Papa came home on his monthly furloughs, he would inquire about my report cards. But his real concern was whether or not I had been in trouble. They were both so worried about getting out that they gave little thought to my studies.

"Always remember," Papa told me, "those Communists are just waiting for you to make the slightest mistake. And when you do—wham! They'll take that visa away as quick as you can blow out a candle. All my time in this work camp will have been for nothing, and you, hijo, will be going into the army."

"Papa, don't say that!" I begged him. Any mention of the military terrified me. I was eleven now, and there were rumors that because the draft age was fifteen, the authorities were stopping the visas of any family with a boy over fourteen years and six months. That shaved half a year off the time we could afford to sit around waiting for the telegram. Fourteen still seemed like a long way off, but I had learned that the more you want time to slow down, the faster it seems to fly by.

"I'm telling you, guys," I said to Luis, Tito, and Rolando one day as we lounged outside the Jagua Movie House, "the day before I'm fourteen and a half, if we haven't got that telegram yet, I'm going to steal an inner tube and jump into the water."

"Yeah, right," said Luis. "The sharks will be nibbling on your liver within the hour!"

"Is the army really that bad?" Tito asked. "Sometimes I think I might join when I'm old enough."

"It's one thing if you want to join," I said. "It's another if they force you."

"Man, am I bored," said Luis. "Can't go anywhere, can't do anything. What are we supposed to do, just sit around here and go crazy?"

At that moment, Rolando nudged me and nodded.

"Look who's coming," he said.

It was La Natividad, the crazy lady, wearing all black as usual. She was walking down the sidewalk toward us.

"Oh, brother," groaned Tito. "Watch out! She's going to turn us into frogs!"

We all waited to see what La Natividad would do. She crossed the street so she wouldn't have to come near us, giving us a dirty look.

"You see that? She acts like we're a bunch of criminals," complained Luis. "What have we ever done to her?"

"Man, she gives me the creeps. Every time I see her, she's talking to herself," I said.

"That's because she's casting magic spells," Rolando said darkly.

"She talks to demons, too!" added Tito. "I swear, that lady is a witch!"

"Of course she's a witch! Everyone knows that," I said. "Sometimes I can smell some weird kind of smoke coming from her house. She does black magic ceremonies, I think."

We watched as La Natividad reached her house at the end of the street and opened her creaking iron gate. Then she climbed the dozen or so steps to her front door and went inside. Her house was big and spooky, and she kept her shades drawn all the time. Wild, thorny plants had taken over the yard decades earlier. A mango tree also grew there, its branches heavy with plump fruits. Dozens more were rotting on the ground.

"Look at that! What a waste!" said Rolando. "Here we are on bread and water, and that old hag has a yard full of perfectly good mangos. I'm going to get me some right now."

"Go ahead," said Tito. "I'd love to see that."

"Wait until she goes out again," Luis advised. "If she catches you, she'll make a drum out of your skin!"

"She goes out every night around dark," said Tito. "If you do it then, we'll go with you."

"She's into Santería, you know," I said.

Santería was a strange, ancient religion, so powerful that even Fidel left it alone. A combination of black magic, voodoo, and various African rituals brought by slaves long ago, it involved drums, chanting, and animal sacrifice. I had seen many Santería ceremonies with my own eyes, and heard many more. The *santeros* held their services in a vacant lot near San Carlos Street, always late at night. When they really got going, I could hardly sleep for all the howling and pounding.

"No way am I messing with a *santera*!" said Tito.

"I don't believe in that stuff," I said. "Those people are crazy. They don't have any real power. If they did, they would have turned Fidel into a frog long ago."

"Fidel is afraid of them," Luis said. "That's why they're still allowed to have their ceremonies. Which just goes to show you how crazy he is. I'm not allowed to go to church school anymore, but these people can sacrifice chickens under the full moon? Does that make any sense at all?"

Luis's words sparked an idea in me. If Fidel really was afraid of the santeros, maybe I could gain some kind of power over him by breaking into La Natividad's house and stealing one of her magic charms! I had no idea what a magic charm looked like, but I figured I would know one when I saw it. And if I was successful, then perhaps, just perhaps, it would give me the power I needed to liberate my family from the grip of this madman.

"I bet I could sneak into her house and steal something before she comes back," I said.

"Look who's such a big talker," said Rolando.

"Dare him! Dare him!" said Luis.

"Good idea," said Rolando. "Calcines, I hereby officially dare you to break into La Natividad's house tonight while she is gone, and if you don't do it, you are the biggest chicken in Cienfuegos."

"I accept," I said.

"Now we're going to have some action!" Tito said, rubbing his hands together.

"How do you know she's going out tonight?" said Luis.

"She goes out every night," Tito said. "I have no idea where, or for how long, but I can guarantee you this—it has something to do with the Devil. Of that, I am positive. Just ask anyone. They'll tell you."

There was silence as we pondered this weighty information.

"So we'll have to move fast," said Tito.

"We? What is this 'we'?" said Luis, alarmed.

"Well, if Calcines is going, I'm going," said Tito, "and if I'm going, my brother is going, and if we're going, you're going, Luis."

"I see," said Luis. "In that case, I'm going home now to say my prayers, because tonight is the night we die."

That evening, the four of us watched from behind the fence around my yard as La Natividad came out her front door, then went down the steps and through the gate. As usual, she was wearing all black, and she was clutching a large, shapeless black bag. Even stranger, on this night she held an umbrella over her head—even though it was dark out, and not a drop of rain had fallen in days! It was such an odd sight that fingers of fear began to tickle my spine.

"Man, she really is nuts!" Luis whispered.

"Shh! Quiet!" said Tito. "She can hear a frog croak a mile away."

"She can see the freckles on a frog's ass a mile away, too," Rolando said. "Keep it down until she's gone."

La Natividad looked around. She was always suspicious of everyone and everything, but she seemed especially on guard tonight. I wondered if she'd sensed us. Then she moved on, disappearing around the corner.

The four of us swung into action. We ran down the street and flattened ourselves against the wall until we were sure no one was watching. Then I pulled on the rusty old gate. As I'd expected, it was locked.

"Great," I said. "We have to go over the wall!"

La Natividad's property was surrounded by a concrete wall about six feet high. Once there had been iron stakes stuck in the top of it, but a lot of them had rusted and fallen out over the years, leaving gaps that a boy could wiggle through.

"What about her dogs?" whispered Luis.

"Oh, yeah!" said Tito. "The dogs!"

"How could we have forgotten about the dogs?" Rolando said, slapping his forehead. "What are we, idiots?"

La Natividad's dogs were two large, vicious black mutts, with yellowed, dripping fangs and beady, malevolent eyes. They were one of the many reasons we usually didn't walk near La Natividad's house. If we did, they would come charging up to the gate and bark madly until we were gone. But she must have left them in the house, because there was no sign of them in the yard.

"Well, over we go," said Tito.

The four of us hoisted ourselves over the wall and dropped to the ground on the other side. There, in front of us, were the mangos, some of them rotten, others as fresh as if they had just fallen that day.

"Look at them all!" said Luis. "Wow, do they look good!"

"I wonder if they're cursed," Tito mused.

"Well, I'm starving," said Rolando. He was about to bite into one, but I stopped him.

"Listen, man, every fairy tale I've ever heard about witches starts just like this," I said. "Some kids are about to steal the gold, but they see some food, and they stop and eat until they're as fat as pigs. Then the witch comes back and cooks them!"

"You're right," said Rolando. "I've heard those stories, too."

"Good thinking," said Tito.

"We'll get the mangos on the way back. Let's go up and try the door."

"Oh, man, Calcines, I don't know." Rolando groaned. "Maybe this wasn't such a great idea."

"You were the one who dared me!" I said. "You can't back out now. If you do, you have to wear a dress to school every day for a week." That was the punishment we had devised for anyone who backed out of a dare. So far, it had never been enforced, but we took it very seriously.

"I'm not wearing any dress!"

"Then let's go," I said.

We slunk like ninjas up the crumbling concrete steps, until we were at La Natividad's front door. I could smell some strange odor, no doubt the smoke lingering from one of her magic ceremonies. It was an exotic, intoxicating scent.

"Wow," I whispered, turning to face the boys. "Whatever this lady is up to, it's something really—"

"Yaaaaaaaaagh!" screamed Luis, falling backward down the stairs.

I whipped around to see what had frightened him so. The front door had opened, and there stood La Natividad, leering horribly down at us. Behind her, I could see two slavering sets of jaws, and I heard the sound of guttural growling.

"It's her! She flew back on her umbrella!" Tito yelped.

I said nothing. I was too busy running. I leapt down the stairs four at a time and headed straight for the wall, but I wasn't moving fast enough to escape the dogs, one of which was right behind me. I could feel its hot breath on my calves as I dived for the wall and pulled myself up. A pair of fangs grabbed my shorts and refused to let go. I kicked madly behind me until I heard a yelp and a thud, and then I was over.

Catching my breath, I looked up to see Luis sitting beside me.

"How did you get here so fast?" I asked, astonished.

"Fear," he answered.

Tito and Rolando were not as lucky. Luis and I could hear their pathetic screams blending with La Natividad's screeching as she urged the dogs on. Suddenly their heads appeared above the wall, and they, too, dropped onto the sidewalk. Tito was bleeding from a gash on his leg. Rolando had lost his pants.

"Run!" Luis yelled.

We needed no further urging. New speed records were set as we disappeared down San Carlos Street. We didn't even bother saying goodbye as we escaped into our houses.

Somehow, I was able to make it through the front door and into bed without Mama hearing me. But as I lay there pretending to sleep, I could hear La Natividad's dogs barking, furious at having lost their chance to sink their teeth into our bottoms. After an hour, they settled down, but I knew that I could never go within a hundred yards of that house again.

How had La Natividad gotten back into her house without our noticing? She must have used witchcraft; there was no other explanation. It occurred to me that she might have a back door, but I dismissed that as too commonplace. I could more easily believe that she'd flown through the air than that she'd gotten the drop on us by sneaking around the block.

If I was going to escape Fidel, I thought in frustration, then it would have to be without the help of La Natividad's magic charms.

As the barking faded, there came another, even more ominous sound. From the vacant field nearby, I could hear a drum start up, followed by chanting and the beating of a tambourine. The santeros were at it again. I was sure that La Natividad had summoned them to cast a magic spell on us. I waited all night for some demon to come slinking through the window and steal my soul. But I must have fallen asleep, because the next thing I knew, it was morning, and I was still the same old troubled boy, waiting for his telegram to come.

Nguyen Van Troy

One day I looked at the calendar, and I realized we'd been waiting for our telegram for nearly a year. The suspense was starting to feel like a wasting disease. I could feel it taking another little bite out of me each day. The worst part was that I couldn't even talk about it with anyone. Mama and Esther felt the same way, so there was no point in complaining to them.

"Complaining only makes things worse!" Mama would say, and Esther would get upset if she saw that I was upset. I couldn't talk to the boys about it, either. They talked about nothing but my impending escape to freedom. I was sick of their wild speculations about blond girls, hot dogs, and apple pie. So I kept my agony to myself.

Papa continued to slave away at the work camp, month after month. He was one person I didn't want to complain to. Compared to what he was going through, my life was like an amusement park. He said the guards were always threatening to take away his furloughs, but so far that hadn't happened. We looked forward to those weekends with tremendous yearning, for we missed Papa fiercely. Each time we saw him, he looked thinner and more exhausted. But Papa had not earned his reputation as one of the strongest men on the docks of Cienfuegos for nothing. He had the endurance of a draft horse, and he swore that he would not let the Communists beat him down.

"Look at it this way, hijo," he said during one of his visits. "We may not know what day that telegram will arrive, but God knows. And every day that passes brings us one day closer to that moment."

"But I want to know when it's coming!" I said. "And what if they don't send it at all? What if they forget or they just decide not to let us go?"

Papa drew me close and gave me a bone-crushing hug.

"Sometimes the hardest thing about life is not knowing," he said. "Not just about this, but about everything. It's not an easy lesson, but you'll have to learn it, son. M'entiendes?"

"Yes, Papa, I understand."

Just before school started, the Caballero brothers and I decided to make a trial run to Nguyen Van Troy Middle School, which was much farther than Mariana Grajales—at least a mile and a half. To get there, we had to cross through the territories of three or four gangs. We wanted to find a safe route. Luis would have been with us, but he'd had a bad asthma attack and was stuck in bed.

Rolando was very quiet and I thought it was probably because he hadn't been promoted. Rolando was an even worse student than I was. The thought that he was going to have to spend another year in sixth grade was eating him alive.

"Ah, don't worry about it, Rolo," I said. "Who cares anyway? At least you don't have to walk so far."

Rolando snorted. "Who the hell is Nguyen Van Troy, anyway?" he said. "What kind of dumb name is that?"

"He's Chinese," said Tito.

"No, he's Russian," I said.

"That's not a Russian name," said Tito.

"Well, one thing's for sure. He's a Communist. Probably some kind of hero or something," said Rolando.

"There are no Communist heroes!" I said.

The brothers instinctively looked around to see if anyone was listening. Then Tito turned to me. "Calcines, if you want to get your butt thrown in jail, that's your problem. But leave us out of it."

"Sorry. But it's true. They renamed all these schools after people we've never heard of, and they expect us to care? What's wrong with our own Cuban heroes? We have plenty of them!"

From Papa's stories of Ritica la Cubanita, I knew an assortment of tales dating from the war against the Spanish colonialists. For the rest of our walk, I regaled the boys with anecdotes about José Martí, Antonio Maceo, and Carlos Manuel de Céspedes, men of dignity and courage who had sacrificed everything to free us from Spanish control.

"How do you know all this stuff?" Rolando asked. "You can barely read!"

Far from insulting me, Rolando's comment jolted me into a realization: I *was* capable of learning—as long as it was something I was interested in.

"I just don't care about learning the crap those Commies are always trying to shove down our throats," I said. "I know the *real* history of Cuba. All they teach us in school is lies and more lies."

We arrived at Nguyen Van Troy without getting into any fights. I stared solemnly at the crumbling brick edifice that would be my new home for the next three years . . . or until the telegram came. There was no way it could take *that* long. With a shudder, I realized that if it hadn't come by the time I finished ninth grade, I'd be too old to leave the island. The army would have its claws in me then. My old, familiar fear began uncoiling from my belly like a snake and crawling up through my chest. With an effort, I pushed it down again, willing myself to be a man and not a boy.

That school year dragged on just like the year before it. In early 1968, Abuelo Julian went to the sugar mill and came home near the beginning of the summer, and we rejoiced that he was safely with us once more. School ended. I had learned that Nguyen Van Troy was a Vietcong soldier who died fighting against the "evil Yankee empire." Now every morning I met up with Tito, Rolando, and Luis on the front steps of the Jagua Movie House. We sat around and tried to think of stuff to do that would be fun but wouldn't get us into trouble. It was a short list. We went to the port, we spied on La Natividad, and went on long countryside walks to the cemetery. Because there was so little we could do, summer, which I yearned for throughout the school year, seemed like a different kind of prison sentence.

Then one day, as the boys and I were sitting around in the stultifying heat, a soldier in a jeep appeared out of nowhere, pulled up in front of our house, and handed Mama a piece of paper.

The boys and I looked at one another, then shot to our feet. The instant the soldier drove off, all the neighbors flooded our front yard.

"The telegram!" someone shouted.

My heart stopped. Was this it? Would we be leaving one week from today?

But Mama opened the envelope, then shook her head. "It's not the telegram!" she said to the crowd. They dispersed, disappointed.

"What is it, Mama?" I asked, out of breath.

"It's Papa," she said.

My heart sank like a stone. Esther came up behind Mama, clinging to her skirt. "Is he—is he okay?"

"It's his hernia," she said. "It's gotten worse, and he will have to have an operation."

"What? It's that bad?"

"Well . . . it's not great, but at least he'll get to come home for the surgery. And afterward, he'll have some time off to recuperate."

"You mean Papa will be able to stay with us for a while?"

"Yes," said Mama. "Papa is coming home."

"Yay!" Esther and I jumped for joy.

But then I stopped. "Mama, if the Communists think Papa is such a bad man, then why are they doing this for him?"

The look on her face told me she was thinking the same thing. I waited to hear what kind of glass-half-full reason she would come up with this time.

"Because," she said finally, "your papa is such a hard worker they think he's worth repairing. Even the Communists can see what a good man he is."

I had to hand it to Mama. Sometimes she actually convinced me that everything was all right.

When Papa got off the bus a few days later, the three of us were waiting for him. I was shocked at how sick he looked. His skin hung on his bones like a badly made suit. He walked bent over, because of his constant pain. We brought him into the house, laid him in bed, and gathered around him.

"Oh, they're trying to work you to death!" exclaimed Mama. "Those animals! They're no better than Nazis!"

"It's okay," Papa said. "The important thing is, I'm home."

"Papa, are you really having an operation?" I asked. "Are they going to slice you open and look at your guts?"

"Niño!" said Mama.

"Eww!" said Esther.

"Yes, they are," Papa said. "And they're going to sew up my hernia so it doesn't hurt anymore."

"Is it going to make you all better?" Esther asked.

"It's supposed to," Mama said. "Now, you two scoot so your father can get some rest. He needs it."

Later that night, as I lay in bed, I could hear their anguished voices. Mama had the same fear I did: that the Communists were going to use this operation as an excuse to kill Papa on the operating table. It would be a quick and convenient way for them to dispose of a troublesome worm. All it would take was a few too many drops of anesthetic.

"We can't worry about every little thing that pops into our heads,

Concha," Papa told her. "What will be, will be. Right now, the important thing is I'm home with my family again, and this operation means I will have a nice long break from that horrible place."

"If you survive it," Mama said bitterly.

I was surprised—she never let herself voice such dark thoughts in front of us kids. She was so good at hiding them that I'd almost come to believe she didn't have any.

"Enough of that kind of talk," Papa said. "You don't know how good it feels to lie down in my own bed with you again, and to know my little ones are safe and sound in the next room. If you did, you wouldn't be carrying on about what might happen. You have no idea of the things I've seen, Concha. I've told you only a tenth of what really goes on. I am never going to tell you about the rest, ever. They're too sad and horrible. But I'll tell you one thing right now—I'm either going to get my family to America, or I'm going to die trying. And whether I die on the operating table or in front of a firing squad, it's all the same. This Revolution is going to fail, Concha. It might take a long time, but someday Fidel Castro will be dead, and the truth about what has happened here will come out. And then the world can hang its head in shame for not having tried hard enough to stop it."

The day before his operation, Papa bade us goodbye, as nonchalant as if he were going to the store. Mama went with him, leaving Esther and me with Abuela Ana and Abuelo Julian. Esther wailed as the taxi pulled away.

"Shh," said Abuela, "don't cry. Your parents will be back soon, and your papa will be as good as new."

"Yeah, Esther," I said—though I didn't believe it. "Everything will be fine."

"I'm hungry," Esther whined.

"Me, too," I said.

"How about some chicken soup?" Abuela said. "I'm sure Eduar would love to help me make it."

"No way, Abuela!" I said. "Forget it!"

Abuela started laughing and I knew she was thinking about the last time she had made chicken soup for us. Abuela had decided that at the age of twelve, I was old enough to learn how to kill a chicken. She handed me a broom and told me to use it to corner a chicken, then grab it and wring its neck. I must have chased that chicken around the yard for an hour, until it finally gave up, out of a combination of exhaustion and terror. I grabbed it by the neck, but the thought of killing the poor bird was just too much. I gave it to Abuela and she handed it back, telling me to twist its neck three times until I felt it break. I lost courage before I could make the third twist, and I let the chicken go. It fell to the ground and began to flop around, as chickens do when they are dying. Then, suddenly, it got to its feet and took off again. I begged Abuela to let that be the end of it, but she handed me the broom again without a word, and I knew what I had to do. After another endless chase around the yard, I captured it again. Under her firm gaze, I finally managed to do the chicken in. I could not eat a bite of the soup she made from it, and I never wanted to kill another chicken again.

"Well, if not chicken soup then let's make ant bread!" Abuela suggested.

Esther and I stared at her.

"Ant bread?" I repeated.

"Sure! You can make bread out of anything," Abuela said. "Even ants. Isn't that right, Julian?"

"Absolutely," said Abuelo. "I often had ant bread when I was growing up. As a matter of fact, I like nothing better."

Abuela took us into the kitchen and opened a drawer.

"Look inside," she said. "What do you see?"

We looked.

"Ants," we said.

"Precisely. Now, I am going to take these ants and grind them up."

"Disgusting!" Esther said.

"No, watch, you'll see. First, though, I need a little flour. Lucky thing I bought some yesterday from the lady who supplies your mama. Esther, get me the flour, please. Eduar, go fetch the molasses. I have a little I've been saving."

We did as we were told. We watched, spellbound, as Abuela mixed everything together, but we didn't see any ants going in. Finally, I couldn't stand it any longer. "Abuela, you've got all the ingredients together, and there still aren't any ants in it!" I said.

"Well, what do you know?" Abuela said. "Whenever I'm short on ingredients, I use ants to fill in, but it looks like I didn't need to add them this time. Well, maybe next time."

I was old enough to know that I'd been had. But Esther hadn't quite figured it out yet. When the pumpernickel bread was ready, she stared at it for a long time, then wrinkled her nose. "I don't like ant bread," she said, and no amount of cajoling from either Abuela or Abuelo could get her to eat it.

"I guess that's like me and chicken soup," I said to Abuela.

Papa's Homecoming

Even though I was, as Abuelo had said, practically a man now, I spent many of the following days waiting for Papa in my childhood sanctuary, whistling to the birds and daydreaming about the future. Would I move to America and become a baseball player, as Abuelo had assured me? Would I perhaps meet and marry a Hollywood movie starlet, possibly even becoming a famous actor myself? Or would I grow up to bring peace and prosperity back to Cuba?

The time passed even more slowly because I knew Papa was truly at the mercy of the Communists now. I imagined him surrounded by evil doctors with big, bushy beards, their white gowns stained with the blood of other innocent Cuban fathers. I cried myself to sleep at night, hoping no one would hear me and tell Papa that I was nothing but a wimp, after all.

And then, three days later, they came back. Esther saw them first.

"They're home!" she cried, watching from Abuelo and Abuela's front window. I raced to her side and looked out. Mama disembarked and held her hand out for Papa, who started going up our steps slowly, still weak, but already looking more like himself. Remembering Mama's instructions that we were not to jump on him, we ran across the street toward him, yelling, "Papa's home! Papa's home! Papa's home!"

He greeted us with gentle hugs.

"My beautiful kids," he said. "How glad I am to see you again!"

"We're glad to see you, too," I told him.

"We had ants for lunch!" Esther said.

"Let me guess. Ant bread." Papa smiled.

When I saw that smile, I knew everything was going to be okay. For a little while, at least, I had my papa back.

Later that day, I sat in his bedroom, looking at his scar.

"So," Papa said casually, "have you got a girlfriend yet?"

I felt the roots of my hair burning. "No!" I said.

"You sure? You're blushing."

"No, I'm not!"

"You'll be starting eighth grade soon, so I guess I'd better ask you this. Do you know about the birds and the bees?"

"The who and the what?"

"How babies are made, I mean."

"Oh, man," I groaned. "Papa, you're embarrassing me!"

Papa grinned. "All this time I've been away, all I could think about was how many things I wished I had time to tell my son. Now that I'm home, you're too embarrassed to hear it?"

"Papa, I already know, okay? The man and the woman get naked and lie in bed together, and then—"

"Yes?"

"Well, you know!"

"No, I don't know."

"But you and Mama made me and Esther!"

"Yeah, but I think I forgot how it goes," Papa said. "Remind me."

"Papa, *please*!"

"There's nothing to be embarrassed about, Eduar. It's perfectly natural. It's how all children are made. The man—"

"La la la la la!" I yelled, putting my fingers in my ears.

"—and then—"

"La la laaaaaaa!" I screamed.

"And then the man's seed fertilizes the woman's egg, and nine months later, a baby comes out."

"Are you done?" I asked, removing my fingers.

"Yes, I'm done."

"Thank God," I said, hopping off my chair. "I'm going to go outside for a while, Papa, and when I come back, I hope these thoughts are out of your head, because it's not healthy for a man to lie around all day thinking such things."

"Eduar, my niño," said Papa, obviously trying not to laugh, "soon enough you will find out that a man thinks of almost nothing else!"

Up to that time, it was true, girls had not been much on my mind. But Papa's little speech must have set something in motion, because suddenly I could think of nothing except girls, girls, girls. Specifically, one girl. Her name was Deborah.

All the boys at Nguyen Van Troy Middle School were crazy about Deborah. She had a certain something that distracted us and made our breathing grow shallow. At least, that was the effect she had on me. Her jet-black hair, her soft, dark eyes, and her wonderful girly smell—hard to explain, but utterly captivating, falling somewhere between flowers and fresh bread—made me a blithering idiot whenever she was around. I'd been feeling this way for some time, but I hadn't understood that it had anything to do with birds and bees. I just figured something was wrong with me. Now, I realized that maybe this was the same feeling that had come over Papa when he sang "Dos Gardenias" to Mama. Maybe Deborah was going to be my Conchita.

"I'm going to ask Deborah on a date," I told the boys one day as we lay like a bunch of alley cats in the sun in front of the movie house.

"For real?" Tito asked. "Just like that?"

"Where will you take her?" Luis asked.

"Here," I said. "To a movie."

"Take her to a romance!" Rolando suggested. "That will put her in the mood."

"The mood for *what*?" Luis asked.

"For the birds and the bees!" said Tito, laughing.

"Don't talk about my woman like that," I told him. "Speak with respect."

"Hey, relax, Calcines! She's not your woman yet! You haven't even gotten up the nerve to ask her!"

"Well, I'm going to."

"When?"

I hadn't actually made concrete plans yet, but now that I'd opened my mouth, I could see I was going to have to back up my words with action.

"Today," I said.

"This we've got to see!" the three of them said in unison.

Deborah lived in a housing complex about a mile from San Carlos Street. That afternoon, the four of us ventured there together, waiting around in front of the building until she appeared, carrying a basketful of rice from the bodega. I was very happy to notice that Deborah smiled when she saw me. I was less happy to realize that my knees had suddenly become watery.

"You clowns stay here while I go talk to her," I told the boys.

Traveling the twenty feet or so to Deborah was the longest walk of my life. Afterward, I couldn't even remember what I said. I was so nervous that I blocked the whole incident from my memory. All I knew was that somehow Deborah agreed to meet me at the Jagua Movie House that weekend for a matinee showing. I went back to the boys in triumph, my feet scarcely touching the ground.

"You really did it," Tito said, awed.

"Calcines has a date!" howled Luis.

"Congratulations, man," said Rolando, slapping me on the back. "I didn't think you had the nerve! Now you're going to be the first one of us to take a girl out!"

"Are you going to kiss her?" demanded Luis.

"Of course I'm going to kiss her," I said. "You guys can come along and learn from the master, if you want. I'll show you how it's done."

I didn't dare say a word about my date to anyone in my family, because Mama and Esther would have just embarrassed me—*How cute! Eduar has a date! Smoochie smoochie!* Even Papa would have teased me about it, and I didn't want anything to ruin the way I was feeling. At the appointed hour, with my hair slicked back and my face scented with aftershave—even though a razor had yet to touch it—I waited outside the Jagua Movie House for Deborah. I had already bought our tickets with money I had begged from Tío William, who thought I was going to the movies with Luis. Deborah showed up right on time. She looked so beautiful in her white dress, clearly cleaned and pressed for the occasion, and with a flower behind her ear, that I felt my face get hot.

"Hi," I said. "You look great."

"So do you," said Deborah.

She stood there smiling at me, while I wondered if maybe now was the time to kiss her. But that would be moving too fast. Instead, I presented her with her ticket, and we went inside and found our seats just as the show began.

Since the early days of the Revolution, only Communist-approved movies were allowed in Cuba. Most of these were terrible Soviet productions, featuring unbelievable cheeseball plots. But I didn't care. I'd chosen a romance, as the boys had suggested, because I fully intended to kiss Deborah—and not just on the cheek, either. It was going to be on the lips, just like in the movies.

Meanwhile, my three buddies were seated five rows behind us. I'd already warned them that if they made a peep or embarrassed me in any way, I would rearrange their facial features. They were impressed enough by my having a date with an actual girl that they agreed to stay cool.

Now it was time. Somehow, I had to get Deborah to let me kiss her. During the first few minutes of the movie, I put my arm around her—not her actual body, mind you, just the back of her chair. The tips of my fingers brushed the ends of a few strands of hair. That was great progress—real, physical contact. I hoped the boys were taking notes.

But for the next two hours, I tried again and again to summon the courage to lift my arm up around her shoulders, only to lose heart every time. I could practically hear the seats creaking as the boys leaned forward to see if I'd made my move yet. Finally, with the film almost over, and the big, climactic on-screen kiss just seconds away, I realized that it was now or never.

My arm had fallen asleep long ago. I couldn't even feel it. I picked it up somehow, draped it over her shoulder—at least, I think I did; it was so numb I could hardly tell—and, just as the Russian hero on the screen leaned in to kiss the starlet, I puckered up, Deborah turned to face me, and—

"Niño!" came a shrill voice.

I groaned. It was like a bad dream.

"Eduardo Francisco Calcines! Where are you?"

Ripples of laughter passed through the audience. I could hear the usher pleading with someone.

"Ma'am! Ma'am, you can't just barge in here like this! Ma'am, can I please have my flashlight back?"

"Just a moment, young man," snapped the voice, which could only belong to one person. "I'm here for my grandson, and when I find him, I'm going to take him out of here and burn his butt. You'll get your precious flashlight back, don't you worry. Do you really think an old lady like me is going to steal it? Niño! Where are you?"

I could hear the stifled snorts of the boys. I made myself as small as possible. Abuela went from row to row, shining her flashlight in the face of each and every moviegoer, calling my name. Everyone found this very amusing.

"Niño!" total strangers yelled, imitating Abuela's voice. "Eduar! Get home right this minute!"

"I think your grandmother is looking for you," said Deborah.

"I want to die," I muttered.

Finally, the beam of light found me. A clawlike set of fingers latched onto my earlobe and pulled me out of my seat.

"How dare you go to a movie without letting your parents or me know!" Abuela said, loud enough to be heard in Havana. "You tell your little girlfriend that if she wants to see you anymore, it will have to be in the backyard, because you are grounded, Eduardo! Now, let's go!"

Abuela marched me down the aisle, chiding me and yanking on my earlobe all the while, and pulled me out into the blinding sunlight of the real world. My protests fell on deaf ears. She towed me down the street to my house, where she delivered a full report to my parents. Mama was upset, so Papa didn't dare say anything. But I caught him winking at me, and when no one was looking, he silently mouthed the words *Good job!*

The next day, my wings were clipped. I was told I could stay at home or go to Abuela's house, but nowhere else. Sitting up on my rooftop sanctuary, I was whistling out my pain to the birds when I heard Abuela's voice.

"Well, young lady, what a nice surprise! Eduardo is in the back. You can go out this way."

I could hardly believe it. I scrambled down the avocado tree in time to see Deborah come out the back door. So she didn't think I was a loser, after all! If only the boys were here to see this moment!

"Hey," I said.

"Hi, there," she said. "You're really good at those bird calls."

"Sorry about yesterday," I said.

"That's all right," she told me. "It wasn't your fault. I had a nice time."

"I was afraid you didn't."

"Don't be silly," she said, and then, without warning, she leaned forward and fulfilled the dream that had been thwarted by my grandmother. Her lips tasted like heaven. When she finally pulled back, I thought I was going to faint.

"Wow," I said.

"Glad you liked it," she said. "I've never kissed a boy before."

"Me, neither," I said. "I mean—what I meant was—I've never kissed a girl before, either."

"I knew what you meant, silly," said Deborah. "I have to go now. My mama thinks I'm at my uncle's house."

"Can I come see you when I'm not grounded anymore?"

"Sure," said Deborah, smiling.

Things were going so well, I decided then and there to take the plunge. "Do you, uh—wanna be my girlfriend?"

She smiled even more broadly. "Yes!" she said.

"Well . . . great!" I said. I didn't know what to do next, so I held out my hand and we shook, as if concluding a business arrangement. Then, laughing, we kissed again.

"See you soon, Eduardo," said Deborah.

Then she went back into the house, politely saying goodbye to my grandmother and grandfather as she left.

"Well," said Papa when I told him all about it, "it seems we had our little talk just in time. So you have a girlfriend now!"

"I guess so." I tried to keep my chest from exploding.

Papa smiled—barely. He'd been home for three weeks, and he was fully recovered from his surgery. I'd gotten used to having him around all the time again, and Esther and Mama and I had been pushing the inevitable out of our minds. But I could tell from the expression on his face that he had something bad to tell me.

"What is it?" I asked.

"I have to go back," Papa said quietly.

"When?"

"Tomorrow." He showed me the piece of paper that had been delivered earlier that day, ordering him to report back to the work camp or face time in prison.

I nodded. I really wanted to cry, but that would have felt stupid after the events of the last couple of days. I was no longer a small boy. I wanted Papa to know he could depend on me to keep things together while he was gone.

"Maybe they won't work you so hard now," I suggested.

"They might not," said Papa. "Then again, they might." He shrugged. "One way or the other, niño, we're a day closer to getting that telegram. Don't forget that. Promise?"

"I promise, Papa."

The next day, the three of us waited with him at the bus stop until that belching, overloaded piece of junk finally pulled up. We hugged Papa goodbye, then watched as the bus went down the street and turned the corner. Then, without another word, we went back inside the house.

Señora Santana

"Which one of you is the worm known as Eduardo Calcines!" screamed the short, plump woman at the head of the room. "Stand up now!"

As dead silence settled over my math class, I stood next to my desk. The eyes of my classmates were on me like laser beams. But they were nothing compared to the steely gaze of Señora Santana. It was my first class of the day, and I'd been an eighth grader for all of ten minutes, but already she'd made it her mission to humiliate and frighten me.

"You are Calcines?"

"Yes, señora."

"Well, then, you are a worm."

I said nothing.

"Your parents are worms, too! I hear your father is being taught by our leaders how to be a useful member of society, instead of a worthless, leeching parasite. If you're in such a hurry to leave Cuba, why don't you go jump in the water right now! Go on, swim to your beloved America, you Yankee-loving worm!"

I stood in silence. I was almost used to this kind of treatment. But I'd had high hopes for this year, and as I realized it was just going to be more of the same, my heart began to sink. How much more of this could I stand?

Señora Santana, like many Cubans, was of African descent. She wore a ponytail that pulled her hair tight against her skull, and her eyes gleamed with the fervor of the truly brainwashed. Her appearance was made even more terrifying by the electrical tape that held one arm of her glasses to the rest of the frame. Her beloved Communists couldn't even provide her with a decent pair of glasses. She was so caught up in the glory of the Revolution that she didn't see the irony in this. Those broken glasses were a subtle sign that even though the Revolution was a failure, she wasn't going to acknowledge it. In other words, she'd abandoned reason and common sense. What made this most frightening was that she had total authority over me. I was once again in the hands of a zealot.

"Well? Do you have anything to say for yourself?"

"I'll show you who's a worm," I muttered.

"What? What was that?"

"Nothing, señora."

"You were talking back! How dare you! Go to the corner and kneel!"

As I knelt in my shorts on the bare linoleum, Señora Santana roughly pulled my arms out to the sides and turned my palms up. Then she put a heavy book on each hand.

"If those arms fall one inch, I will beat you until you can't sit anymore," she said. Then she waddled back up to the front of the class.

"The rest of you, take out your books. No looking at Calcines, unless you want to join him!"

"What happened to you today?" Luis asked.

"Nothing. Just these damn Communists are trying to kill me, that's all."

"Señora Santana, huh? I could hear her yelling all the way down the hall."

"She's crazy. The other teachers just ignored me, but she really has it in for me. Go on and tell me about how good Communism is while I'm eating hard bread and sugar water to fill my hungry stomach at night. Give me the Yankees and the land of the free any day!"

The boys got quiet after this outburst. I did, too. I was afraid I had gone too far. But then Tito spoke up.

"You're lucky you're getting out of here, Calcines," he said, keeping his voice low.

Abuelo was always telling me to look for the sunbeam among the clouds. With the darkness so oppressive, it was easy for me to forget that light had ever existed. But a couple of days into my new year of hell, I found my sunbeam. Her name was Olga. During the summer, Deborah and I had fallen out of love as quickly as we had fallen in love, and had decided to just be friends.

Olga was half Cuban and half Chinese, a mixture that had resulted in a creature of stunning, exotic beauty. Her skin was light, her hair black as night. She was slender and elegant, and her dark eyes were almond-shaped, like a movie star's. My embarrassment at Señora Santana's treatment had been so acute that it had taken me a while to notice her in that class. But once I did, I pushed Santana into the background, until she became nothing more than a yammering recording that played over and over, like one of Fidel's speeches.

I'd seen Olga before. She'd been standing in line one day in the barrio of Tulipán, the neighborhood where Tío Amado lived. I was on a bus, coming home from one of my panetela runs. Even though I'd only seen her for a few moments, her face had etched itself into my mind, and I'd thought about her all the way home. And now, here she was, not only in the very same class, but sitting right next to me!

It took me a couple of weeks to work up my courage, but finally I approached her on the playground one day.

"Hi," I said. "You're Olga?"

"Yes. And you're Eduardo."

"I think I've seen you before. You're from Tulipán?"

"I live by the curve in the road with all the mango trees. You don't remember me?"

"I saw you outside a store once last summer."

"No, I mean from before that. You've been to my house, silly!" She looked around, then leaned over and whispered in my ear: "My father is the one who sells tropical fish."

I was shocked. This was *that* girl? Dimly, I remembered meeting a skinny little waif that long-ago day when Papa had taken me to get a fish as a reward. But never in a monkey's age would I have connected that girl with Olga.

"Wow!" I said. "You've changed!"

Olga smiled.

"So have you," she said.

"So . . . your dad's a Communist?"

She rolled her eyes. "Yeah," she said. "And you're not."

I laughed. "You could tell, huh?"

"It's too bad Santana is so hard on you. Nobody likes her, you know."

"Ah, she's nothing," I said. "I can take whatever she dishes out. Anyway, if you don't mind my asking . . . do you have a boyfriend?"

Olga smiled again, then blushed.

"No," she said.

I looked her straight in the eye and smiled.

"Good," I said. Then I winked, and thank goodness my eyelid didn't get stuck.

"I can't believe you have a new girlfriend already!" Tito moaned.

"What can I tell you? I'm unstoppable," I said.

"Does she know you're a dissenter?" Luis asked. He sounded worried.

"Of course she knows! The whole school knows!"

"But her dad . . ."

"Ah, forget her dad. I know things about him. He's not such a great Communist. He's just playing along until Fidel gets killed, or something."

"Watch out, Eduar," said Luis. "There's no way this can last. Olga's a Communist, too."

"Not even Communism will protect her from my manly powers," I said. "I keep telling you, boys—watch and learn."

"Oh, we'll be watching all right," said Tito.

"Anyway, I can't walk home with you guys anymore. I have to walk with Olga from now on."

"Yeah, well, you better wear good shoes," said Luis. "You're gonna have to do some serious running if you're coming home alone. Some of those barrios you have to pass through are pretty tough."

But that didn't worry me. I would have fought a hundred kids a day for the privilege of walking with Olga.

For the next few months, Olga and I met after school every day. We walked and talked about everything under the sun. Our afternoons together were like a balm for my soul. They eased the pain that Señora Santana caused me in the morning. And the longer I spent with Olga, the more I fell in love with her, and the more I yearned to stay in Cuba.

School let out for winter break and resumed in early January. I hadn't been able to see Olga all that time, because my parents had wanted me to stay around the house. I didn't mind. We were a complete family again, and it felt great.

Papa's hernia hadn't healed properly, and the Communists had finally decided to give him lighter duty in Cienfuegos. His task now was to walk the streets with a broom and dustpan, sweeping up trash. Far from finding this humiliating, Papa was thrilled. It was much easier than his labors in the cane fields. Best of all, he got to come home every day at five o'clock. Between this and my love affair with Olga, it seemed that maybe life in Cuba might be bearable, after all.

But when I saw Olga again after the break, I could tell that something was wrong. The look on her face was distant, and when I tried to take her hand, she pulled away.

"What's the matter?" I asked.

"I have to tell you something," she said. "I can't be your girlfriend anymore."

"You have another boyfriend?" I asked. "Who is he?"

"No, it's not that. My dad says I can't see you."

"But why?"

"He's been getting more serious lately. He wants me to join the Party. I'm going to start going to Young Pioneer meetings. And to be honest, Eduardo . . ." She paused a long moment, then continued. "I really think you're doing the wrong thing by giving up on our Revolution. You have to give it a chance. Better days are just around the corner. If only everyone would pull together and allow El Comandante to complete his work without getting in his way . . ."

Her voice trailed off as our eyes met. I shook my head in disgust. Then I turned and walked away.

"I'll kill him!" I raged to my grandparents.

Abuelo Julian and Abuela Ana were sitting in their living room, listening to me rant. I paced up and down before them, clenching my fists, trying not to cry.

"I'll rip his liver out and eat it!" I said.

"Who are you talking about?" Abuelo asked.

"Who do you think? The man who has ruined our lives! The man who's taken over everything and is tearing our country apart!"

"Ah. You mean Fidel."

"Yes, I mean Fidel!" I said. "And I don't care who hears me!"

"What happened in school today, niño?"

I told them. As I repeated Olga's words, their true import sank in—

she had chosen Communism over me. I could hardly believe it. Was all that time we'd spent together, sharing our feelings and talking about a future together—was all that just a game?

"Eduar, you are so young. Your heartache will pass, and you will meet the woman of your dreams when you're ready," Abuela said.

But I wasn't having any of it. I ran into the back room and grabbed the picture of Fidel from where Abuela had kept it overturned ever since my late cousin Peruchito had given it to her. I brought it into the living room.

"This is what I'm going to do to him!" I screamed. I raised the picture over my head and threw it to the floor. Then I stomped on it over and over, as tears flowed down my cheeks. "I'm going to kill him!" I began screaming all the filthiest playground language I could think of. I had never spoken this way in front of my grandparents before, but I had reached my breaking point. I couldn't take it anymore. And they seemed to understand. Normally, I would have felt a spoon on my bottom, but this time they just listened.

When I'd finally calmed down, Abuela went and got the broom, and Abuelo leaned forward in his chair. "Look me in the eye," he said.

I looked.

"I want you to remember one thing, Eduardo Calcines. Long after I'm gone, I hope you hear these words in your head whenever you start to feel again the way you feel right now. Killing solves nothing. Killing Fidel would solve nothing. There will only be another Fidel to take his place. Fidel is not the problem. Fidel is a symptom."

I stared at him, not understanding. Fidel wasn't the problem? How could that be?

"Fidel is a symptom of the problem," Abuelo said again. "The real problem is not sitting in Havana, smoking a fat cigar. The real problem is here." He tapped his chest.

"You mean . . . you have a bad heart?"

"No, no. I mean the *human* heart."

"He doesn't know what you're talking about, Julian," Abuela said as she swept up the broken glass. "Put it in plain language."

"I'm talking about evil," said Abuelo.

"So am I!" I said.

"Yes, I know. But what I'm saying is that if you give in to these feelings, niño, you are no better than they are. Killing Fidel makes you the same as Fidel. Hating the Communists makes you the same as the Communists. Nothing will be solved by killing, niño. If you kill Fidel, or anyone else, the Communists win, because they have made you like them—a murderer."

"That makes no sense at all, Abuelo."

"Someday it will," he said.

"Remember the words of Our Lord, niño," said Abuela.

"Which words?"

"All of them," she said. "But especially what he said about committing murder in your heart. If you do that, then it's the same as doing it for real. So don't commit murder in your heart. I understand you are angry. We have all suffered, my boy. But as your grandfather says, if they make you like them, they win. Don't become a killer. Don't become angry. Stay the fine young man that you are. That's how you will beat them."

"Look, I'm sorry, but neither of you makes any sense at all," I said. I wiped my cheeks on my arm and sniffled. "My girl just dumped me because I'm not a Communist! And one of my teachers says horrible things about me every day in front of all the other kids! Papa was taken away from us and now he has to shovel crap in the streets! We don't have enough to eat! Tell me how killing Fidel wouldn't help! Explain it in a way that makes sense!"

"You're thirteen, and soon you will be a man," Abuelo said. "So it's important for us to have this talk now, while your mind is still fresh. Let my words sink in, niño. Even if you don't agree with them, carry them inside you. You will have to make a choice someday, boy. It's up to you."

"If it were up to me, I'd truss Castro like a pig and roast him over hot coals!" I shouted.

Then I ran out of the house and climbed the avocado tree up to the roof so I could sob my heartbreak among the birds.

Time passed, and my wounded heart healed little by little. But I became consumed by thoughts of getting Olga back. I had to bide my time. If only she could see me do some of the things I was good at—play baseball, or something! I would have to be on the lookout for a chance to show her what she'd given up.

Meanwhile, my grades plummeted. Señora Santana delighted in pointing this out in her class whenever I failed an exam. Somehow, in her mind, stupidity and dissent were the same thing.

"What an idiot you are!" she crowed one day in March. "You'll never amount to anything, Calcines."

But later, on the playground, I checked my exam against one of my classmates'. Although our answers were nearly the same, my score was forty points lower than his.

"I can't believe this!" I told the boys on the way home. "She's not even being fair!"

"She really has it in for you," said Luis. "Lucky for you we're being sent out to the country for a while."

I stopped in my tracks. "We're what?"

"It's the Schools-to-Countryside program," Tito said. "Didn't you hear the announcement?"

"He's too busy daydreaming about how to get Olga back," said Luis.

"Shut up," I said. "What's going on?"

"We're all going out to an onion farm for a month to help with the harvest," said Tito. "It's gonna be fun!"

"Fun, yeah," I said. A pang of fear shot through me. I'd never been away from home for that long. "How do we know they're not just going to keep us there forever?"

"They wouldn't do that to kids," said Luis.

"Oh, yes, they would," I said. "I don't trust them at all."

"It's an adventure," said Tito. "I'm looking forward to it."

Suddenly, a sunbeam burst through the clouds. "Are the girls going, too?" I asked hopefully.

"Ha! Listen to him!" Luis laughed.

"Yes, Olga will be there, too," said Tito.

"Perfect!" I said. "This will be my big chance to win her back. She'll see me working like a champion, and she'll fall all over me."

"Yeah, because every girl wants an onion farmer for a boyfriend!" Luis howled.

Our school had been ordered—or "selected," as the Communists preferred to phrase it—to pick onions in the mountains around the city of Trinidad, about a hundred miles from Cienfuegos. Mama and Papa packed me a suitcase full of nearly everything I owned. I could see that they were worried and trying not to show it. It was becoming all too familiar for the Calcines family—an enforced separation from loved ones to provide the government with free labor.

"It's going to be cold in the mountains," Mama said. "So dress warm."

"Don't forget to brush your teeth," Papa said. "And do as you're told. Don't make trouble."

"It's only a month," I said, hiding the urge to throw my arms around them. "At least we know I can come home when it's over."

"That's right. And you'll be another inch taller the next time we see you," Mama said.

The bus stopped and I got on. I waved out the window until we turned the corner. Then I pushed all thoughts of home from my mind. It wouldn't be so bad in the coming month. I'd have Tito and Luis to hang out with, and maybe another shot at impressing Olga. I began to get excited. Work? I could handle a little work. I was more interested in what kind of fun we were going to have.

It started that very night, after we'd all arrived at the farm and been sent to our bunks. The boys and girls had separate barracks, and Tito, Luis, and I managed to get beds next to one another. This was a recipe for disaster. Also, the temperature was around forty degrees Fahrenheit, which was the coldest weather I'd ever experienced. With only onion sacks for blankets, there was no chance of falling asleep. We laughed and talked until midnight, when some other kids started throwing things at us to make us shut up. This turned into a massive brawl, with the air full of flying articles of clothing and toiletries. The man in charge came stomping in, wearing his pajamas.

"All right!" he shouted. "You want to play games, let's play games! Everyone strip down to your underwear and fall in! Everyone! All of you! Let's go!"

We did as we were told, wondering what strange punishment he was about to inflict on us.

"Now! Out the door—march!"

Out into the frigid night the fifty of us went. Luis was in front of me, Tito behind. We cursed as our bare feet encountered soggy, cold mud.

"No slowing down! This will teach you! Double-time! Let's go! We'll see how much screwing around you do then!"

We marched for what seemed like all night. I knew before twenty minutes had passed that Luis wasn't going to make it. He'd begun to wheeze and cough so badly that I was scared for him. By the time we got back to the barracks, thoroughly chilled and covered in mud, he was in the middle of a full-blown asthma attack, and the doctor had to be summoned.

The rest of us collapsed in our bunks and fell asleep. In the morning, Luis's things were gone.

"He's going home," Tito informed me. "And I wish I were going with him. Some adventure this turned out to be."

"I wish I were, too," I said.

The front door banged open, and there stood our tormentor.

"Everybody up! Let's go! Fall in for breakfast, and then let's get to work!"

Breakfast was a steaming pot of white beans. We could see the worms in it. I remembered Papa's stories of the conditions at the work camp. This place was no better. I wondered how on earth he'd survived living like this.

We worked all morning, picking onions out of the mud. At lunch, we got another bowl of wormy beans. In the afternoon, after we'd knocked off for the day, we were herded into a large horse pen and hosed down until most of the mud had dripped from our bodies. Dinner—another bowl of beans. Then bedtime. I'd caught a single glimpse of Olga as she worked with the girls, but I was so exhausted I couldn't even bother looking a second time. My interest in her had dissipated. All I could think about was my empty stomach and my aching back.

"We have to escape," I said to Tito that night. He sat cross-legged on his bunk, eating a raw onion.

"How?" he said. "Where would we go?"

"Anywhere."

"They'd catch us before we got a mile."

"So? What are they going to do, execute us?"

"Maybe not, but how impressed will Olga be if she hears you ran away?"

I didn't even bother replying to this.

"You're going to be sick," I said. "Eating raw onions is a surefire way to get diarrhea."

"No, it isn't."

"Just you wait."

"That lucky bastard Luis," said Tito. "I wish I had asthma." Suddenly, with a panicked look, he shot to his feet and headed for the outdoor latrine.

"I told you!" I yelled after him. But I was too tired to laugh. I lay on my bunk and stared up at the rafters. About an hour later, Tito reappeared, looking white and shaken.

"Oh, my rear end," he moaned.

"Stick an onion in it," I advised him. "That will keep everything inside."

"Calcines, I have to tell you something."

"What?"

"Promise me you won't tell anyone? I'm really worried."

"Promise."

"When I was sitting in there, I looked down at my—my you-know-what."

"How did you see it without a magnifying glass?"

"Quit screwing around. I'm seriously worried here. I saw something . . . *growing* down there."

I became alarmed. "What are you talking about?"

"Uh . . . well . . . I'm getting hair."

"Oh, that," I said. "That's normal."

"You're getting it, too?"

"Sure," I lied. "I've had it for months."

"Wow. Thanks! I was afraid there was something wrong with me."

"There is," I said, "but not that."

I would have flung a few more barbs his way, but I was so tired that I fell asleep before I could say another word.

The following Sunday, after we'd been there a week, we were given some time off. Tito and I walked toward a nearby river, on a dirt road that led away from the onion farm. We kicked stones and told each other stories.

"You know, I used to have a lot of big dreams," he said. "I wanted to be a sports hero or a millionaire. But you know what I want more than anything now?"

"What?"

"I just want a job and a wife. A couple of kids, maybe. Nothing special. That's all. That's not too much to ask for, is it?"

Under Castro, it might be more than you'll ever get, I almost said. But the look on his face was so hopeful that I couldn't tear him down.

"Sure, you can do that if you want," I said. "You can do anything, Tito. Castro can't stop you."

"That's right!" he said, his eyes bright with excitement.

Why not let him dream? He knew he had to stay. I wanted nothing but happiness for Tito. But this desire was made all the more poignant by the fact that in a country where getting ahead was illegal, he would have a very hard time achieving even these simple goals.

A Taste of Freedom

It was a hot, humid day in late June 1969. The boys and I lounged in front of the Jagua Movie House. The heat shimmered madly above San Carlos Street, as if the very asphalt were on fire. Moving our limbs was a major effort. As usual at this time of the month, the last of our rations had run out. Mama now had a hard time coming up with one meal a day, so all of us were on sugar water and hard bread until the first of July, when we would have the privilege of standing in line for three or four hours to collect our canned horse meat. I no longer dreaded the taste of the stuff. I actually looked forward to it. At least it was protein.

"Look at Benao," said Luis. "How come he always has so much energy?"

We all turned and looked at the mailman as he came marching down the street, chipper and spry in his freshly pressed uniform.

"That's why they call him 'Deer,' " said Rolando. "I bet he gets extra rations."

"Man, I'd hate that job," I said. "How would you like to walk around town in all this heat?"

"You'd like it if you were getting extra food!" Rolando said.

"That would depend on what I got."

"How about a nice big slice of roasted pork with congris?"

"I want a cheeseburger, like they eat in America!"

"Oh, shut up!" Luis groaned, holding his stomach. "Why do you guys always talk about food? It drives me crazy!"

"Hey, Calcines!" said Tito. "I think Benao is going to your house!"

We all sat up and looked. The mailman was crossing my yard, a letter in his hand.

Suddenly, I had plenty of energy. "I'll be right back!" I said. But the boys all got up and ran across the street with me. We rushed to the front door just as Mama and Esther appeared.

"Gracias, señor!" Mama called after Benao. Then she held the letter up and looked at it.

"It's from America!" she said, her voice shaking with excitement. "From Milwaukee!"

"That's where Tía Dinorah is!" shouted Esther.

"Open it, Mama!" I said.

"All in good time," Mama said. This was not our first letter from Tía Dinorah, but we hadn't gotten one for a while. Besides, every letter from America was something to be savored. The four of us boys trooped inside and sat on the floor, as if it were story time. Esther sat primly on the couch. Mama arranged herself on the rocking chair, smoothing her apron over her lap. Then she held the letter up to the window.

"There's a letter inside, and there's something else, too," she said. "They put a little present in there for you kids, I think. It's long and thin and rectangular, and it's—"

"It's gum!" I yelled, getting up and dancing. "They sent us a stick of gum! Open it, please, Mama! You're killing me!"

"I don't know. Maybe I should wait until your father comes home," Mama said.

"Aaaagh!" the five of us kids yelled.

"Relax, I'm just kidding." Mama slit open the envelope with her finger. "It's gum, all right," she said, holding it up. "Juicy Fruit!"

"Mama, let us have it!" Esther said. "Please, please, please!"

"No, you have to wait until I read the letter first."

"Read it out loud!"

"Let's see. 'Dear Concha, Felo, and kids. This is just a short note to let you know that we are doing well. Arturo's job is going well in the metal fabrication plant. We moved to the second floor of a beautiful home, in a nice neighborhood called West Allis. Our block is lined with big oak trees that reach the sky, and when it snows and the sun shines, they glow like they are covered in diamonds. You will love it here. There are giant hams in the supermarkets, and you don't even have to wait in line to buy them! We miss you and hope that your telegram will come soon. We talk about you every day. Hugs and kisses to everyone, especially my dear parents. Love, Dinorah.' "

Mama held her apron to her nose and closed her eyes. We waited for her to compose herself. Then, with a sigh, she folded the letter and put it in her apron pocket.

"I must go read this to Abuela at once," she said. "Now, here's the gum. Niño, I leave it to you to divide it fairly."

"I will, Mama."

Mama went out the front door. I tore the gum in half. One half went to Esther, who held it to her nose and smelled it.

"Mmm!" she said. "I never thought it would smell so good!"

"Go ahead, Esther, chew it," I said. The four of us watched as Esther experienced chewing gum for the first time in her life. The expression on her face went from curious to pleased to rapturous. I wished I had a camera.

"Oh, hermano, I could chew this all day!" she said. We all laughed.

"What about the other half, Calcines?" said Tito. "Are you gonna—"

"Relax," I said. Carefully, I tore the remaining half stick into four equal pieces, and handed one to each boy. They held them solemnly in their palms until I was ready. Then we popped them in our mouths all at once.

"Freedom!" said Rolando. "That's what this gum tastes like."

"You said it," Luis said.

"Man, I forgot how good Juicy Fruit is," Tito said. "Can you imagine what it must be like for American kids? They can go buy a pack of gum whenever they want!"

Our jaws worked on our minuscule treats, and my mind drifted. American gum. Giant hams. No lines. Nice neighborhood. Papa would have a good job. I wouldn't have to defend myself every day—at least, not for being a dissenter. I wondered if American kids ever got into fights. Probably not, I decided. In such a rich country, why would anybody need to fight over anything? Americans were probably the happiest people on earth. I bet they walked around with full stomachs and big smiles on their faces all the time.

"How can freedom have a taste?" Tito asked.

"If it does, it tastes like this," Luis declared.

"I wanna go to Fort Jagua," Rolando announced, out of nowhere.

We all looked at him in surprise. El Castillo de Jagua, or Fort Jagua, had been a favorite destination for families, mine included. There was a beautiful beach club next door, called Rancho Club, which was open to the public. Once in a while, on weekends, Mama and Papa had taken me there, and we'd spent the day swimming and playing. Then our freedoms had been whittled away one by one, and such trips had become too expensive and too difficult.

"Just like that?" demanded Tito. "Suddenly you wanna go to Fort Jagua?"

"You're not allowed!" said Esther to me. "Mama and Papa said you have to stay home, Eduardito. You can't leave the street."

"She's right," I told the boys. "I'll get in big trouble."

"If you get caught, you mean," Rolando said.

"What do you mean, *if*? Between Abuela and Esther and Mama, of course I'll get caught. I can't even blow my nose without someone making a full report on it. And why do you wanna go all the way to the fort all of a sudden?"

"This freedom gum is going to Rolando's head!" Tito said. "It's giving him crazy ideas!"

"I just feel like going," Rolando said. "It might be the last time we all get to go together."

This statement settled over us with a somber weight. Something about the way Rolando was acting made me believe he was right. His sense of purpose was contagious.

"All right," I said. "I'm in."

"Me, too," said Tito and Luis.

"That's it! I'm telling," said Esther.

"Esther, did I or did I not just give you half of that entire piece of gum?" I said.

"Yes."

"Well, then, what a way to repay me! If you tell on me, I'll never give you another piece of gum as long as I live!"

Esther's mouth began to crinkle. "But I don't want you to get hurt!" she said. "Mama says it's not safe anywhere!"

"Nothing's going to happen if we stick together," I told her. "Don't tell anyone where we've gone, m'entiendes? We'll be back by dark. If they ask, we're playing baseball in the field."

"They'll know I'm lying." Esther hiccuped. "And lying is a sin! Don't make me lie, hermano!"

"Fine, don't lie, then. But don't tell them the truth, either."

"That's the same as lying!"

"Esther," said Luis, "what are you, a lawyer? Come on, *prima*. Cut us a break here."

"Don't worry, Esther," Tito consoled her. "With four of us, we'll be all right. And we're not going to do anything bad. We're just going on an adventure. That's all."

"If you're not back by dark, I'm telling!" Esther said. She flounced out of the room.

"Man, she's only nine, and already she's got your butt whipped into shape, Eduardo," Luis said in wonder.

"Women start their training young," said Rolando. "Now let's get going!"

To get to the fort, we had to take two separate buses to the docks, then catch one of the two ferries that ran out to the tip of the peninsula, which encircled the Bay of Cienfuegos like a protective arm.

No one gave us a second glance as we paid our fares with pocket change and went up to the second deck, which offered a grand view of the turquoise bay and the deep blue sea beyond. We sat facing the open ocean, enjoying the smell of the salt air and feeling the fresh breeze on our faces.

"Now, this is more like it," said Tito. "Better than sitting around and sweating to death all day!"

"That water looks good enough to dive into right now," said Luis.

"Go ahead," I said. "It's full of sharks."

"And ghosts," added Rolando. "This bay is haunted by a pirate. Didn't you know that?"

The rest of us made noises of disbelief, none of them particularly polite.

"Tell us another one," said Tito.

"It's true! He drowned right here in a shipwreck, in this very bay! Every time there's a storm and his bones get disturbed, he sinks a ship and takes the passengers down to the bottom of the bay with him. And instead of going to heaven, they have to stay down there for all eternity!"

"Stop it!" said Luis, shivering and laughing. "You're scaring me!"

"Just don't ever get caught on this bay in a storm," Rolando advised us.

"I'll make it a point not to," I said. I worked to keep a tone of derision in my voice. At the same time, I scanned the horizon anxiously, looking for the slightest hint of thunderclouds. But the sky was a perfect, clear blue, with not a wisp in sight.

The fort was next to the beach and a source of endless wonder for curious boys. Papa had told me it was built by the Spanish long ago, to protect their colony from pirates. Now, though it was a crumbling stone ruin, it was still an imposing presence—and a haunted one, too, if the legends were to be believed. Being impressionable, we believed all of those ghost stories: about the headless Spanish nobleman; the weeping bride in the white gown; the soldier in old-fashioned armor, pacing back and forth on a rampart that no longer existed.

But our fear of encountering such phantasms was dissipated by the bright sun and fresh breeze. My friends and I spent the afternoon scrambling around the gloomy old castle, trying to scare one another and hoping to find treasure. We chomped at the slivers of gum from Milwaukee long after the flavor was gone—to spit them out would have been sacrilege. Luis fell and skinned his knee. Tito and Rolando got into a fight, and I had to pull them apart. We ignored the grumbling in our bellies with practiced discipline and forgot about the time. It was the perfect day, and it ended all too soon. As we rode the ferry back, I realized I wasn't going to make it home in time to beat the sunset. Not even close.

As if reading my mind, Tito said to Rolando, "It's the spoon for us for sure, hermano."

"Me, too," said Luis.

"We're all gonna get it. So what?" I said. "It was worth it."

The boys nodded in agreement. We sat facing the stern of the ferry, watching our wake unwind as the sky turned a deep purplish orange.

"We ought to hijack this boat and turn it around," Rolando said suddenly. "There's four of us. We could overpower the captain and throw him over. Then we head for Florida!"

The three of us froze. I couldn't believe my ears.

"Would you shut up?" Tito whispered furiously. "If anyone hears you say that—"

"I don't care. This is insane. I don't want to live like this any more! I want to get off this damn island and go to America!" Rolando yelled.

The three of us looked around in a panic. Mercifully, we were alone on the upper deck.

"You better watch it," I warned Rolando.

"We're not going to America," said Tito.

"But I want to go!"

"Every night now he says this to our parents," Tito told me and Luis. "They've given up trying to beat it out of him. Now they just yell at him and lock him in his room."

"I'm not a traitor. All I want is to be free!" said Rolando. "What's wrong with that? Why does that make me a bad person?"

I'd known Rolando had his gripes about the hardships we all suffered, but for him to say this out loud was heresy. He was the son of a Party member, after all. His whole family would be in deep trouble if the C.D.R. heard about this outburst—and on public transportation, no less!

"Rolando, I wasn't sure you felt this way," I said.

"Well, I couldn't tell you before. I had to keep quiet about it. But now I have the feeling you'll be going soon, Calcines. That's why I wanted to come out here today. We're not little kids anymore. It's the last time the four of us will have this much fun together."

"Come on, man, what are you talking about?" said Luis. "It's not like he's going tomorrow or anything."

"I have a feeling, that's all," Rolando said. "I can see the future."

"Here he goes again," said Tito, rolling his eyes.

"No, it's true," Rolando insisted. "Calcines is going to get out of here. Luis, too. But you and I, hermano"—he shook his head—"the only way we'll ever make it to freedom is if we try to escape. Our parents will never apply for a visa. Even if they did it now, it would be too late for us. It wouldn't come before we're drafted."

"You never know what could happen," I said. "Maybe Fidel will die of a heart attack tomorrow. Maybe the Americans will invade again."

"Yeah, keep dreaming," Tito said. "My brother is right. The only way we'll ever get out is to sneak out."

"You were kidding about hijacking the boat, right?" said Luis. "Because you know what would happen if we did that, right?"

"Okay, so that wasn't such a great idea," said Rolando. He got quiet, and stared out at the water, clenching his fists and gritting his teeth. "If this Revolution is so glorious, then why are people risking their lives to get out of here?"

It was the question that hung over us all the time. But no one dared to voice it. Simply to think such a thing was a crime against the government. You could get twenty years for a thought like that. I didn't believe the Communists had figured out a way to read minds yet, but I had no doubt they were close.

"I wish Fidel were dead," I said. It seemed that if I was ever going to say it, this was the moment.

"I wish," said Rolando.

"We all wish," said Tito.

"What do you want him dead for?" Luis asked. "You're getting out of here. You'll be safe."

"Look at what he's done," I explained. "Our lives are ruined. We live like prisoners in our own country. We have no freedoms. We have no food, man. People can get sent to prison just for complaining about being hungry. We're all doomed to be drafted, and if that happens, our lives will be misery. Life used to be good in Cuba. Now it's worse than bad. And it's Fidel's fault!"

The other three nodded. It was the first time we had ever spoken so openly with one another. A deeper bond was being forged between us. Rolando had been right—it was a good idea for us to come out here today.

"Just don't forget us when you get to America, Calcines," Rolando said. "Try to send us stuff if you can. Gum. Comic books. Stuff like that."

"And see if you can get a tortoiseshell comb," Tito said.

"A what? What the heck do you want that for?"

"I don't know. I just do." Tito shrugged, looking embarrassed. "I read about it somewhere, and it seems like it would be a nice thing to have."

"Okay, a tortoiseshell comb it is," I said, laughing.

"Great. Now, remember, no one says a word about what we've talked about today."

"No way," said Luis.

"You don't have to worry about me blabbing," said Rolando.

"Hey, Rolando. When you look into the future, what do you see for yourself?" I asked.

Rolando didn't say anything. I looked at him to make sure he'd heard me.

"Rolando?"

“I don’t know what I see,” he said quietly. “Just . . . nothing.”

We fell silent again, listening to the throb of the boat’s engines and watching as the setting sun painted the sky, then faded into blackness.

Late that night, my rear end still sore from its recent encounter with Mama’s hairbrush, I lay in bed, staring up at the ceiling. Despite my richly deserved punishment, I was in a reflective, almost peaceful mood. It had been an important day. Something had shifted, and I felt different. Rolando said he saw me in America, living life to the fullest. I still could not even imagine what kind of person Eduardo Calcines would be if he became an American. I couldn’t imagine anything about my life at all. Here I was, about to enter the ninth grade, and I had no dreams or aspirations for the future except to get out of Cuba. Beyond that, everything was just as blank as Rolando had said his own future was.

Suddenly, I heard shouting from Tía Silvia’s next door. I recognized the voice of my cousin, Oscar, raised in anger. I sighed. They were at it again.

Tía Silvia’s family, like so many, was torn about whether they should stay or go. She and my tío were considering leaving, but their son, Oscar, wanted to stay. Neither of them could understand why he would want such a thing, and it had become the subject of nightly battles, all of which we could hear through our open windows.

“I can’t leave!” Oscar screamed now. “I want to go into the international forces and spread Communist values of fairness and equality throughout the world.”

"Listen to him!" my uncle said. "He sounds just like those idiots on the radio!"

"Oscar, please, listen!" pleaded Tía Silvia. "Don't you understand? It's all a bunch of lies! You're just going to end up getting killed in some godforsaken place, and no one will even know where your grave is! Is that what you want? You want to sacrifice everything for nothing?"

"It's not nothing! At least I have goals!" said Oscar. "I have to work with what I've got, not run away like a coward!"

"Running away from Cuba doesn't make you a coward," said Tía. "It makes you a survivor."

"Yeah, right," sneered Oscar. "Listen, if you two want to go, go. Run away with the Calcineses. Maybe you remember better times, but those are long over. This is the reality of my life. You think I want to grow old in a country where it snows every day, and all the people are drunk, fat, and lazy?"

"That's not what America is like!" Tía said. "The people are very nice!"

"They are trying to sucker you with their propaganda!" Oscar said. "Everyone knows that." I recognized some of the things Oscar was saying from the propaganda we were taught in school from the age of five onward. The Communists had done a good job on him. It was as if they owned his mind.

"It doesn't snow in Florida," observed Tío. "Florida is just like Cuba, I hear. Same weather, same everything."

"Yeah, and plenty of wealthy capitalists ready to get rich from your labor," sneered Oscar. "I've learned all about that precious America in school. You know how blacks and Latinos are treated there? Like second-class citizens. You've seen the same footage I have of black people being attacked in the street by the police while they were marching for their rights. Americans have no understanding of equality. The whites have the best of everything. It's everyone else who has to do the dirty work, and get paid almost nothing for it."

"We are white, too," Tío said. "We have European blood."

"Don't you understand? It doesn't matter!" Oscar yelled. "Once they hear that Spanish accent, you can consider yourself lucky if they let you clean their toilets! You think you'll be better off, but you won't! You'll be worse off!"

On and on the battle raged, as it had for the last several nights. I didn't even have to get out of bed to hear every word. I heard the door slam as Oscar stomped out of the house and sat on his porch, crying.

I snuck out of bed and went to the refrigerator, where I retrieved the sliver of gum I'd stored there for safekeeping. I popped it in my mouth, then slipped out the front door and over to Oscar's house.

"Who's there?" he whispered as I approached through the darkness.

"It's me, your cousin."

"Hey, primo."

"Hey. I heard you fighting again."

"Sorry, man. Things are tense right now."

"I know. You really believe all that stuff about America?"

"Well, what do you think? You've seen the same films I have," Oscar said.

We all had seen the footage of what happened to the demonstrators in the civil rights movement—the Communists made sure that it was shown before each and every feature film in the theaters. *Think America is the land of freedom and opportunity? Think again—especially if you have brown skin!*

"Yeah, I know. But it's not like that all the time."

"How do you know?"

I shrugged, but he couldn't see me in the dark, and he took my silence for defeat.

"Look, primo, I don't want to hurt your feelings," Oscar said, "but I really think you and your family are doing the wrong thing. Don't you believe in the values of Communism even a little bit? Don't you at least think there's something good about it?"

"You know what? I actually do think there are good things about it," I said. "It would be nice if everything really were fair. If everyone shared everything, then no one would go without. But look around you, Oscar. That's not the way it is. Everyone is terrified of the government, the military, and the police. No one has enough to eat. And the Communists are a bunch of liars. In Havana, they eat the best of everything every night. The higher up in the Party you are, the more stuff you have."

"Are you saying Communism is a lie?"

I wasn't afraid to say what I really thought to Oscar. He was family. "Yes," I said. "That's just what I'm saying."

I heard the boards of the porch creak as he stood up.

"Then, primo, maybe Cuba really is better off without you and your family," he said. "As long as we have to put up with this kind of thinking from people like you, then we have to be strict. People have to be re-educated to see things the right way. It doesn't happen overnight. It takes years, and sometimes you have to do it by force."

"Right," I said. "Like how my papa had to go to a labor camp. He'd be there still, if not for his hernia. Is that the kind of re-education you're talking about?"

"I always felt bad for your papa, but—"

"Save it," I said, cutting him off. "You know what, Oscar? I think you gave up thinking for yourself. I don't even believe you ever knew how to use your brain. You just swallow all the crap they shove down your throat in school. You're one of them, aren't you? You're just like the people who sent Papa away. You don't care if people get hurt or killed. You don't care if families are torn apart. You're blind. Completely blind."

Oscar was silent for a long moment.

"It's too bad we can't see eye to eye on this, primo," he said finally.

"Yeah, it is too bad," I said. "Maybe if your papa ever gets yanked out of bed by the military in the middle of the night, you'll understand why I don't think this Revolution is so glorious."

We stood in the thick, moonless Caribbean night, barely able to see each other. I chewed my gum ferociously, loudly, defiantly.

"Where did you get gum?" Oscar asked.

"Tía Dinorah sent it from Milwaukee."

There was a long pause.

"Gum will rot your teeth," he said.

I didn't answer.

After a moment, he said, "Good night, Eduardo. And good luck."

I knew by the way he said those words that Oscar and I wouldn't be talking much anymore.

"Good night, Oscar," I said, "and good luck to you, too. And God bless you. You're going to need His help a lot more than I will."

I turned and went back into my house before he could say anything else. I put my gum back in the fridge—I would keep it there for weeks, until it was too flavorless and disgusting to chew anymore. Then I got back into bed and tried to sleep. Oscar had gotten me worked up, and I was mad. But I was sad, too. Our clan had begun to split about ten years earlier, when Peruchito joined the military. Now there were whole families that weren't speaking to other families. Family gatherings, even if they'd been allowed by the government, would have been impossible, anyway. Half the people weren't speaking to the other half.

I grew drowsy thinking about Rolando's words. He'd seen a vision of me in America, he said. And Luis was there, too. We would make it to the land of freedom and opportunity—giant hams, no lines, chewing gum, ketchup, blond girls . . .

With those thoughts comforting me, finally I slipped into my dreams.

Planning to Escape

Saturday, October 4, 1969: my fourteenth birthday. As usual, I awoke at sunrise and stepped outside to greet the soft morning. The songs of countless tropical birds filled the air as the sky became first a fiery red, then orange, then settled on blue. Normally, I would have whistled back to them, but today I had no stomach for it. I felt as if they were singing my death knell.

More than three years had passed since Papa had applied for the visa. On every birthday since then, I'd sworn that the next one would be celebrated in America. I'd even dared to imagine it: I'd have a big chocolate cake with vanilla icing, and maybe even ice cream, too—a delicacy I'd never tasted.

But this birthday was like a bad dream. Even if Mama had come parading out of the kitchen with the most beautiful cake in the world and all the ice cream I could eat, it would have tasted like mud to me. I was six months away from being too old to leave the country because I'd have to serve in the military first, and we were still stuck. I was beginning to believe that the government had simply flushed our application down the toilet. I could picture Fidel rubbing his hands together, cackling with glee. *That stupid Calcines thinks he's going to get away from me? Well, I'll show him that it's not so easy!*

Soon I heard Papa moving about the house as he made himself some of the bitter Russian tea he was forced to drink when our monthly coffee ration ran out and the new jars hadn't arrived. Then he came outside and sat with me on the front step.

"Happy birthday, niño," he said.

"Thanks, Papa."

"Fourteen now! I can't believe it. Soon you'll be a man." He took a sip of tea and made a face.

"Soon I'll be drafted, you mean," I said. "My very next birthday, they're going to come for me. And if that stupid telegram doesn't get here in the next six months, it will be too late, anyway."

Papa shook his head. "No, niño. We'll be gone by then."

"You say that every year."

"This time I mean it."

"You say that every year, too!"

Papa smiled. "You have the memory of an elephant," he said. "Let's not worry about anything today. Just enjoy the feeling of being fourteen. Here, I got you a little something." He reached into his pocket and pulled out an object that he kept hidden in his hand.

I held my hand out. He dropped a crumpled piece of green paper onto my palm. Carefully, I unfolded it and held it up to examine it. "What is it?"

"It's an American dollar bill."

I'd never seen American money before. It looked like a message from a different planet.

"Wow! Where did you get this?" I asked.

"I found it when I was cleaning a street downtown. Someone must have dropped it. I've been saving it for you."

"But where can I spend it?"

"Don't spend it! Save it. Think of it as a good luck charm. If you keep it with you, it will remind you of where we're going. Positive thinking has real power, niño. If you want something to happen bad enough, it will."

"Thanks, Papa."

"You're welcome. So, what will you do today, on your special day?"

I shrugged. "Nothing different, I guess. The boys and I will hang out in front of the theater like always."

"Well, don't flash that dollar bill around. You can show it to your friends if you want, but make sure no one else sees it, especially the C.D.R. Otherwise, you might have some explaining to do."

"Okay, Papa," I said.

But I had no intention of showing the money to the boys. I would keep it safe in my pocket, and once in a while I would touch it, just to remind myself that if Papa hadn't given up yet, then neither would I.

Rolando had failed the sixth grade yet again. He now stood at least six inches taller than everyone else in his class, and the shame he felt at being lumped in with a group of babies when he himself was starting to shave had become too much for him to take. He was starting to act really strange.

"Rolando, man, I don't get it," I told him. "You're not stupid. You're the best chess player around. You can even beat your teachers. What's the matter with you? Why can't you pass the sixth grade?"

"That's easy for you to say," he snapped. "You've got your whole future to look forward to! What reason do I have to study? None!"

"You don't know what the future holds," I objected. "Anything could happen. You just don't know!"

"I don't care what happens," Rolando said. "I just show up to class and sit there. I don't care if I pass or not. I'm going into the army soon, anyway. Maybe I'll kill myself."

"Rolando! Don't say that!"

"What? Who cares? Why shouldn't I? I can starve to death as a civilian or I can get shot as a soldier. Or I can take matters into my own hands. That's my right. It's my life."

"Suicide is a sin!"

"Have you forgotten?" Rolando sneered. "God doesn't exist anymore, remember? Fidel says so. So there is no such thing as sin."

Sometimes I felt as if I didn't know Rolando at all anymore.

At least I was a ninth grader now, which meant deliverance from Señora Santana and her broken glasses. Now I could walk by her classroom with relief instead of dread. True, she still glared at me sometimes from the doorway, but I just ignored her. I had new teachers this year, and though they were just as disdainful of my family's political position, they didn't go out of their way to make my life miserable. I wasn't worth their time. They simply stuck me in the back of the room and forgot about me. That was just fine. I was free to stare out the window and daydream about girls, food, and freedom.

Olga and I barely even glanced at each other in the hallway now. I'd long since moved on. Besides, Olga had joined the Young Pioneers, the Communists' national youth organization, and she wore the bright red neckerchief with pride. To me, that neckerchief seemed like a collar, a symbol of submission. It was like announcing you had given up thinking for yourself. Even if she'd come crawling back to me on her hands and knees, begging me to take her back, I would have refused. I would have been ashamed to be seen with such a girl on my arm.

In the absence of any particularly cruel teachers, life had become tolerable again. October and November passed quickly. Now I had a new date to fear: April 4, 1970. That day I would turn fourteen and a half. I was going to have to begin plotting my escape much sooner than that. There was no time to lose.

I had a plan, so secret I hadn't even told my friends about it. If the telegram didn't come, I would try to escape to America. I would go alone, for never in a million years would I have wanted my parents or sister to attempt such a thing. I didn't want the boys coming along, either. If I was going to die, I didn't want to take anyone with me.

It was impossible for Cubans to get access to good maps, especially maps of America. But there was a globe in one of my classrooms, and I would study it, staring at the tiny sliver of water that separated Cuba from Florida, imagining how easy it would be to cross it. I knew that the current went from south to north, and that if I could just make it far enough out to sea, I could drift to safety. I knew also that I'd have to bring plenty of water, and something to shield myself from the sun. As far as the sharks went, I would just have to trust that they would find better pickings than my skinny little self.

But the one thing I hadn't figured out yet was my flotation device. Would it be an inner tube? Should I try to put together some kind of raft? Everything was in such short supply that it wasn't possible to gather even empty milk jugs or pieces of scrap lumber. The more I thought about it, the more I realized that there was really only one practical solution: I would have to steal a boat. And the only boat I knew of belonged to a kid in my class. We called him Manzana, short for Cara de Manzana, or Appleface, because he spent so much time fishing his face was always sunburned red like an apple.

One day in early December, managing to elude both my family and the boys, I went down to the beach where Manzana kept his skiff. Manzana used the boat to go fishing early in the morning, before school. The authorities allowed him to continue his fishing because he was not quite right in the head—too simple, they felt, to try to escape. The skiff was anchored in a secluded area, and there was never anyone around. If I timed it right, I could slip down to the beach at dusk, weigh anchor, and head northwest. That I had never sailed before in my life was no deterrent. How hard could it be? I would be gone before anyone noticed, the navy wouldn't bother with me if they thought I was a simple fisherman, and I would be in Florida by the next morning. It seemed like a foolproof plan. Now all I needed to do was decide when to go. Part of me said it made no sense to wait any longer. Obviously, the telegram wasn't coming.

But I was scared. Several times I went down to the beach just to look at the boat. Even in the light surf that caressed the shore, it bobbed like a cork. How would it handle in the Straits of Florida? What would I do if it sprang a leak? How would I know which way to steer?

A couple of times, I gathered enough courage to wade out into the surf and rest my hand on the gunwales, wondering if I should just go ahead and do it right then and there. But I couldn't even bring myself to crawl over the side. Why not? What was wrong with me?

Finally, I made my decision. My departure window would be the last two weeks of March. If the telegram hadn't come by then, I would steal the boat and make a run for it.

School let out for winter break on December 19. That Sunday, I went to Abuela Ana and Abuelo Julian's house. Abuela had made a special treat for me called *nata*. This was a dish of cream and sugar, and she could prepare it only when she had fresh milk—in other words, hardly ever. I had loved nata since I was a small boy, and I sat now on the living room floor eating it out of a bowl, scarcely pausing to wipe my mouth.

"You know what today is, niño?" asked Abuelo.

"Noche Buena?"

"No, Noche Buena is on the twenty-fourth. Today is the winter solstice. The shortest day of the year."

"So?"

"So if you listen tonight, you'll hear the santeros starting up again with their drums and their singing. This used to be an important holiday, long before the Communists came along. Long before Christianity, even. The old ones used to have special ceremonies on this day to awaken the sun from its long sleep. They believed that the sun was a god, you see, and they worried that if they didn't make a lot of noise he would stay sleeping forever, and no crops would grow anymore."

"Didn't they notice that the days got longer again even if they didn't have any ceremonies?"

My grandparents exchanged amused glances.

"Well, they weren't stupid," said Abuela. "But their ceremonies were important to them. Just like going to Mass used to be for us."

"Well, Abuela, those days are over."

"Yes, but they will come again."

I shrugged. I had long since given up hoping for change.

"You can still hold important days in your heart," Abuelo told me. "Days such as the birth of Jesus."

"Well, what's the point of that?"

"The point is that even though we may forget Him, He will not forget us, niño."

"Okay, Abuelo!" I said. "I'll keep that in mind the next time I have to spend four hours in line for a loaf of hard bread."

"Good," said Abuelo, oblivious to my sarcasm. "Maybe it will bring you some peace."

"The winter solstice is a time of rebirth," Abuela said. "It's a reminder that everything dies and is born again. And it also means anything can happen, niño. Even those things that you may have given up on."

"That would be great, Abuela," I said. "Thanks for the nata. I gotta be going now."

All this talk of rebirth and hope was starting to give me a headache.

That was a Sunday. The next Tuesday, as it seemed I'd been doing every spare moment of my life since I could remember, I joined the boys on the steps of the movie theater, watching the shadows move inch by inch. We were so bored and sluggish that if Fidel himself had walked by and tipped his hat, we would scarcely have bothered to sit up.

"Here comes a jeep," observed Luis.

"Who cares?" said Tito.

"It's turning down San Carlos Street," said Rolando.

"Big deal," I said. "We've seen lots of jeeps on this street before."

"It's slowing down in front of your house, Eduardo!" said Luis.

I was motivated enough now to raise my head and look. Not only was there a jeep in front of our house, but there was an officer in it, wearing a neatly pressed uniform and a cap with a shiny black visor. He leapt out and marched imperiously to the front door of our house, a piece of paper clearly visible in his hand.

"Oh boy," said Luis. "Oh boy, oh boy, oh boy!"

"Calcines?" said Tito.

"Is that the—" said Rolando.

"Shh!" I said.

I watched my mother come to the door and accept the paper from the officer, who then turned and stalked back to his vehicle. With a roar of the engine, he was gone.

Neighbors began sticking their heads out of their front doors. Mama still stood on the porch, holding the paper. I saw Abuela emerge from her house and scuttle across the street. Mama took a couple of steps out into the yard. Then she fell to her knees.

"Mama!" I screamed.

I was across the street and in our yard in the blink of an eye. Tears streamed down Mama's face. Abuela came rushing to her side.

"Concha! Get up, *hija*. Is it the telegram?"

Mama nodded.

Abuela and I looked at each other in disbelief.

"Okay, okay. Come into the house now," Abuela said as she helped

Mama to her feet. "Don't get the telegram wrinkled or dirty, Concha. Let me hold it for you."

"No!" said Mama. "No, I am not letting it out of my sight!"

"Conchita, Conchita," said Abuela soothingly. "The telegram has come. It is not going to go away again. Come inside, sweetheart."

"Is it the telegram?" cried a neighbor.

At the same time, Rolando yelled from across the street, "Calcines, what is it? What did he bring?"

I turned and yelled as loudly as I could, *"The telegram is here!"*

There was dead silence among the dozens of neighbors who were outside now. Then they erupted into a massive and spontaneous cheer. People flooded the street and invaded our home, yelling, clapping, and dancing for sheer joy. A memory flashed through my mind: Noche Buena, 1961. That was the last time I'd seen the whole neighborhood so happy. The winds of freedom had finally blown my family's way.

Esther appeared at the front door, hands clasped to her face. "Mama!" she cried. "Is it true?"

"My baby girl!" Mama sobbed. "Since you were six years old, we've been waiting for this piece of paper! Esther, we're going to America!"

"Aiee!" shrieked Esther. "We have to tell Papa!"

"Papa is at work," I reminded her and Mama.

"Someone must go tell him right now!"

"I'll go!" said Emilio Pérez from across the street. Like a jaguar, he was off.

Suddenly, I realized Papa's assignment to the work detail was officially over. He had been punished enough for his disloyalty. Now they were letting us go.

We had one week to get ready. Our flight to freedom would take place on December 30. But before that could happen, we still had the military to contend with.

Later that afternoon, the same officer came back. This time he carried a clipboard. As family, friends, and neighbors gathered curiously, he made a great show of strutting through our house, checking off each and every item on his checklist, pushing aside anyone who got in his way. We already knew that all our property belonged to the state. Now he was making sure we weren't trying to steal anything from Cuba.

"Excuse me, señora," said the officer with mock civility as he stood in the living room and pointed up at the blank space above the windows. "My records indicate that there were curtains in this room. Where are they now?"

The whole family held our collective breath as we waited for Mama to answer. We knew she'd given the curtains away to another family who were far worse off than we were. She never thought the curtains would be missed. It hadn't even occurred to her that she was breaking the law.

"I—I—" said Mama. "Well, we—"

"Señora, let me remind you of something," said the officer. "If you gave those curtains away, that constitutes the crime of theft against the state. That makes you a criminal, and that gives me the right to revoke your visa right here and now."

We froze. The panic that gripped me now nearly turned my bowels to water. Was it possible that this evil snake of a man could ruin our dream when we were so close?

"So where are those curtains?" he pressed. "What have you done with them? Who is the criminal in possession of them now?"

"Please, sir," said my father.

"Silence, worm!" said the officer. "I was speaking to your wife!"

Papa clamped his lips together and went into their bedroom. I could hear him praying aloud to Santa Barbara, not caring if the officer heard him.

"Sir, I have to be honest," Mama said. "I—I gave them away."

The officer's eyes grew wide. Then he strode out to his jeep. I went to the window and watched as he sorted through some files in the back.

"I had to tell him the truth!" Mama said, to no one in particular. "He would have known if I had lied!"

The officer was in his jeep for a very long time. Papa's praying grew louder. Mama closed her eyes and clasped her hands. Esther was crying. I didn't know what to do. Finally the officer came back in with another piece of paper.

"Very well, I have decided to make an exception," he said. "But I will only give you two hours to vacate this house. If you are still in it when I come back, you will be arrested and sent to prison. Get out now! And the rest of you people, go back to your homes! It's against the law for more than three people to assemble!" And with that he turned and went back out to his jeep. It roared to life, and he careened through the cheering mob on San Carlos Street.

We spent the next two hours moving the personal belongings we would be taking with us—clothes and toiletries, legal documents, photos—into Abuela and Abuelo's house.

Quco Bemba came running up to me. "Calcines, is it true?"

"Yes, man," I said. "We're out of here."

"Wow! I can't believe it!"

"Me, neither."

Quco dug his toe into the dirt and looked around shyly.

"What is it, Quco?"

"I was just wondering . . . since you're going to America, can I have your shirt?"

I laughed. "Of course, man," I said. "But can you at least wait until we're on our way? I need something to wear for the next week."

"Okay!" Quco smiled. "Thanks, Calcines! I will never forget you, ever!"

"I won't forget you, either, Quco."

Now the hard part began—the goodbyes. For the next five days, a constant stream of relatives and friends trooped through my grandparents' house. There must have been five hundred people, including all my aunts, uncles, cousins, second cousins, all of their spouses and children, all of our friends, friends of friends, various people we barely knew but who wanted to wish us well, anyway, and, no doubt, a few complete strangers who were simply curious. I quickly wearied of shaking hands and accepting congratulations. It was all too surreal. I felt as if we had become royalty or movie stars.

The boys hardly left my side. They didn't want to miss a moment. I knew they were happy for me, but the expression on their faces, especially Rolando's, was almost more than I could take.

"You guys want to get out of here?" I suggested on the day before we left.

"What, are you telling us to leave?" Tito bristled.

"No, no. I mean, let's go somewhere. If my cheeks get pinched one more time I'm going to go crazy."

Luis brightened. "Let's go to the field and play baseball!" he said.

Rolando snorted. "With what? Our only baseball came apart a year ago, and I'm sick of playing with wound-up rags."

"Calcines is going to be able to get all the baseballs he wants soon," said Tito. "Hey, why don't you send us a new one when you get to America?"

"Sure, sure," I said, irritated. All these guys seemed able to think about was how much stuff they wanted me to send them once I was free. "But I'm not there yet, so quit asking me, okay? Seriously, I need to get out of here for a while. Do you guys want to come or not?"

"Let's go to the cemetery and pick mangos," said Rolando. "It's not far, and we can't get into trouble."

We all agreed that that sounded good, so off we went. I didn't even bother telling Mama and Papa. They were too busy talking.

The cemetery was located on an isolated stretch of dirt road leading out to the countryside. Mango trees grew there in abundance, and their fruit was bigger and sweeter than those of other mango trees, including La Natividad's. Naturally, we said this was because they fed off the bodies underground. It was a disgusting thought. But Papa had explained to me that that was just part of the cycle of nature. All dead things decomposed and fed new life, he said. Someday *our* bodies would nourish the earth as well, and in this way we would continue to live on.

We climbed the fence and helped ourselves, sucking on the sweet flesh as we read the dates on the tombstones. A lot of them were very old, and nearly all of them belonged to people who'd died before the Revolution. These people may have known hardships, I thought, but none of them knew anything about Fidel. I wondered if the dead were aware of what had happened since their passing, and how they felt about it. Would they want me to stay on the island and work to make things better? Or would they approve of my leaving?

"Someday Fidel will join you," I whispered to the tombstones. "And then he will be judged, and Cuba will once again be free."

"Calcines is talking to himself," said Luis.

"He's going crazy," said Tito.

"That's what freedom does to your head," said Rolando. "Already he thinks he's sitting in Yankee Stadium, watching Mickey Mantle and Joe DiMaggio."

"Ah, stuff it," I said. A wave of anxiety came over me. What was I doing here? I should be getting ready to leave, not acting as if nothing had happened. "I gotta get back home."

"Why? I thought we were gonna have an adventure!" complained Luis.

"I don't have time. Tía Luisa and Tío Jesús are taking us to a restaurant tonight for a goodbye dinner."

"A *restaurant*?" The boys looked shocked. None of our families had had the money to go to a restaurant for years. I had never even been to one. There was little point—there was no more food to be had there than there was in our bare cupboards. But the very word "restaurant" was exciting and glamorous. "The high life is starting for you already, Calcines!"

"Ah, he thinks he's too good to spend his last day with his friends," said Rolando in disgust. "Come on, let's go." He got up and stalked off.

"Don't worry about him," said Tito. "He's just jealous. He'll get over it."

"I hope so," I said.

But I didn't have time to worry about it. There was just too much going on.

The Covadonga Restaurant was once world famous for its paella, a Spanish dish of yellow rice and various kinds of seafood. In its heyday, former and current U.S. presidents had eaten there, as well as lots of other wealthy, famous people. Now it sat empty and forlorn, falling apart both inside and out—because, like every other business in Cuba, it was run by the state.

The Covadonga was situated on Cienfuegos Bay, near Tía Luisa's house at the port. Through the windows, I could see the beautiful sunset over the turquoise waters. Our dinner came—a big bowl of rice. There was almost no seafood in it at all. We didn't care. We dug in and enjoyed it as though we were at one of Tío William's old Noche Buena parties. The adults chattered away to each other like parrots. I scarcely heard a word. My head and heart were full, and soon my stomach was, too.

As we were finishing up, Papa turned to me and said, "Niño, I want you to look carefully out the window, because this is the last sunset you are going to see in Cienfuegos. Tomorrow we go to Varadero, and the next day we will go to the airport and then north, to America."

At last, the moment came that we had been dreading—the hardest goodbye of all.

It was very early in the morning, and in my memory, my grandparents look just as they do in one of the few pictures I have of them, standing in front of their house on San Carlos Street. Tiny, fierce Abuela, whose body gave birth to so many children, and who became the matriarch of a vast clan; handsome, tall Abuelo, who was so proud of having worked his way out of the fields through sheer determination and ingenuity, and who loved his family more than anything else—the man who'd taught me that the world will respect a man who respects himself. They'd soothed my countless hurts, fed me countless meals, and taught me all they could about everything they believed was important. Most of all, they had loved me unconditionally. From them, I'd learned not just how to survive, but how to thrive. They had helped make me the person I was, and I was a part of them. Saying goodbye was as painful as having a piece of my heart ripped away. And I knew from their expressions that they felt the same. Of their five children who would leave for America, of all of their countless grandchildren and great-grandchildren, we were the closest.

There was no pretending anymore that this was just going to be hasta luego. They were too old now.

I stood before them, wearing the pants and shirt that I had worn to church years earlier, and which Mama had altered to fit me for the momentous trip to the airport. I felt like a dolled-up monkey. My awkwardness was made worse by my absolute misery.

"My boy," said Abuelo, "I want you to remember two things."

"Yes, Abuelo." I could barely speak.

"First, remember that every day is a gift. Each morning, you should greet the sun as though it were your bride. Take pride in your appearance, and behave respectfully to everyone."

"Yes, Abuelo."

"The second thing I want you to remember is that you can be a great baseball player, if only you practice hard enough. In America, one can do anything."

Abuelo's silken, wrinkled hands caressed my face. He put one hand on my head for a moment, as if blessing me. Then he bent down, kissed me, and drew me close. I smelled his aftershave and hair pomade for the last time.

Abuela held me, not speaking, just rocking back and forth. I could feel the warmth of her aged body, her inner fire still strong despite being eighty-one years old.

"Remember," she said, "this is what we wanted for you. We want you to be free, niño. This moment is sad, but . . ." She sighed. "Freedom is worth it, my boy. We fought the Spanish for it once, and someday Cuba will have to fight the Communists for it, too. But not us. Our time is over."

"Will—will I see you again?" I said, gulping back my tears.

Abuela smiled and gently shook her head.

"You never know. Maybe not in this life," she said. "On the other side, yes. But not for a long, long time. You have a long life ahead of you. You are taking the first step on a great journey, niño. And we will be watching you every step of the way."

Then they said goodbye to Esther, who was inconsolable. Next was Papa's turn. He and Abuelo had never hugged before, but now they met in an embrace full of warmth, strength, and respect.

"You've always been good to my little girl, and for that I will always love you, Felo," Abuelo said. "I thank God that Conchita found you, and that you are such a good husband and father."

Papa nodded his thanks, afraid to speak. Then he bent down and hugged Abuela.

"I always knew you would come back from that horrible place and take your wife and children to safety, Felo," she said. "You didn't disappoint us. Truly, the angels are smiling on you. God bless you. Go to freedom now, and don't worry about us. We'll be watching over you always."

Then it was Mama's turn.

My grandparents held their baby girl for a long time, whispering into her ear, stroking her hair, consoling her. When the taxi had pulled up to the curb and we could wait no longer, Papa touched her on the arm.

"Concha," he said.

"No!" Mama said. "It's too hard. I can't do it. I can't!"

Abuela took Mama by the chin and looked into her eyes. "You are going to do it, for the only good reason there is," she said.

"Yes, for your children," said Abuelo.

Mama understood then. She kissed them each once more, then stepped back, sniffling. Without another word or glance, she got into the backseat of the cab. Esther got in next to her. Papa sat in front, next to the driver.

"Let's go," he said to me.

I turned and looked at Tito. He was the only one of my friends to come that morning. Luis had had another asthma attack, and was stuck in bed. Rolando had come over alone at the end of the day yesterday to say goodbye, after admitting that it was going to be too hard for him to see me off. It wasn't that he was jealous. He felt too upset about my leaving, and he didn't want to make a scene. I understood. I told him we would be friends forever, even if we never saw each other again. He liked that. I think it made him feel better.

"Good luck, Calcines," said Tito. "Take care of yourself over there. Eat a hot dog with ketchup for me."

"I'll never forget you guys, no matter what happens," I said. It seemed like a stupid thing to say, but there were no good words for such a moment. It was too hard.

Then I got into the taxi. We drove down San Carlos Street, past a sea of faces and waving hands, and the Calcines family left Cienfuegos forever.

Flight to Freedom

Leaving Cienfuegos was like leaving behind a part of my soul. As the taxi left Glorytown, I tried to look at everything all at once, because I knew I was seeing it for the last time. But it was impossible. All four of us were crying. The taxi was filled with the sounds of sniffling and choked sobs. Even the driver blew his nose long and loud, as if he, too, were caught up in the emotion.

In the blink of an eye, the taxi was out of Glorytown, and in another blink it was at the limits of Cienfuegos, on the main road headed to the capital. Our destination was Varadero Beach, east of Havana. It took over four hours to get there, and it was a journey I tried to savor every moment of—but it has fled my memory completely, except for one sight: *campesinos*, farmers, riding their horses along the ancient trails that the modern highway followed. I smiled, because they reminded me of Papa's stories of his youth, when he, too, had been nothing more than a simple peasant. And now here he was, about to get on an airplane to America.

Then we were in Varadero. As we drove slowly down the wide

oceanfront boulevard, we rolled down the car windows and inhaled the fresh sea air.

I had scarcely ever been outside Cienfuegos. I'd been to Havana twice: once for one of the eye operations when I was an infant, and another time at age seven, when we came to visit one of Papa's sisters. But nothing could have prepared me for the sight of this carefully constructed tourist town. Well-fed people from other Communist countries were walking up and down the sidewalks in shorts and T-shirts, taking pictures and buying souvenirs. The shops were full to bursting with anything you could name—including food. It was mid-morning, and my stomach was rumbling. None of us had been able to eat breakfast, not that there had been much to eat, anyway.

"Look at this place!" I said. "It looks like heaven!"

"You see?" Papa said. "This is how—"

Mama nudged him sharply in the side, reminding Papa that there was a stranger in the car. For all we knew, the driver worked for the C.D.R. It was not too late for the government to change its mind about letting us go. We could still be reported.

"This reminds me," he said instead, "of the time we had to bring you to Havana for your operation, when you were just a baby, niño."

"I remember that!" said Esther.

"You weren't even born yet, Esther," said Mama.

"The nurses at the hospital told your mama that she had to leave for the night. But you know what she did? She hid under your bed and slept there, in case you needed her. That's what a fortunate kid you are, hijo. To have a mama like that is the greatest gift a child could receive. She lay there all night, holding your little hand. In the morning, when the nurses found her, they couldn't believe it. After that, they let her stay as long as she wanted."

I looked at Mama and smiled. She smiled back, or tried to.

"What's the matter, Mama?" I asked.

She shook her head.

"Just tense, that's all," she whispered.

I understood. I feared the same thing she did—that we would be turned back at the last moment. But then I was distracted by the sight of the beautiful sugar-white beaches of Varadero.

"Wow! We don't have beaches like that in Cienfuegos!" I said.

"Ah, our beaches are pretty close," said Papa, ever the proud Cienfueguero.

"Can we get out and walk around?" Esther asked.

"Not allowed, young lady," said the driver kindly. "This area is strictly off-limits to Cubans. Tourists only."

"How can Cuba be off-limits to Cubans?" Papa said.

Mama nudged Papa again. This was exactly the kind of comment that could get us into a lot of trouble. The driver said nothing in reply, but then, apparently remembering we were dissidents and not likely to report him, he nodded, then shrugged his shoulders. I saw his eyes meet Papa's in the rearview mirror as a silent conversation took place between them. I was old enough now to understand—the driver, too, was opposed to the regime. He thought the way we did about Castro and Communism. But after ten years of oppression, the habit of keeping one's thoughts to oneself was too deeply ingrained.

"Cuba today . . ." The driver let his voice trail off. This was the closest most people would allow themselves to come to complaining. Then he changed the subject. "You folks are going to Miami?"

"Yes."

"How exciting! My brother is there."

"Do you want us to take him a message?"

"If you happen to bump into"—he said his brother's name—"tell him you were in my cab today. And we miss him."

"We will make a point of it," Mama said. "It will be the first thing we do." And she got out a piece of paper and a stub of a pencil and wrote down the man's name, checking twice to make sure she had spelled it correctly.

Our first stop was the government inspection office. This proved to be a fancy, white, colonial-era mansion on the beach. The driver pulled up in front of it, and we gawked in disbelief.

"Can you wait for us?" Papa asked the driver. "We have to get our papers checked."

"Of course," said the driver. "I don't have to be anywhere else."

"This is a government office?" I said. "It's the nicest house I've ever seen!"

"You see? It's as I always told you," Papa murmured. "They kept the best for themselves, while the rest of us live in filth and ruin."

"Felo! Shh!"

"Sorry."

"Children, you wait out here," said Mama. "Papa and I have to go talk to the immigration people. Sir, do you mind?"

"Not at all. I have five children myself, and three grandchildren," said the driver.

"We won't be too long. You kids behave yourselves, and listen to this nice man."

Esther and I watched as Mama and Papa mounted the broad marble steps of the building and disappeared behind the massive white doors. I was so impressed with the gravity and majesty of the moment that I decided to follow them.

"Hey, boy! Where are you going? Your parents told me to watch you!" said the driver.

But I ignored him, and he let me go, thinking, no doubt, that he wasn't being paid enough to discipline me.

I worked up my courage and opened the door, stepping inside. If I thought the outside was grand, the interior was ten times more so. A thick, soft carpet covered the floor, while potted plants and revolving fans made the house seem like a palace. Uniformed guards were everywhere, their clothes and hats spotless, their weapons gleaming and deadly. I wondered if they ever shot people in here. The thought was terrifying, mostly because it was so believable. Then I saw that Mama and Papa were talking to a lady at a desk.

"Well, how should I know? That's not my problem, is it?" the woman was saying in reply to something they had asked. Her tone was brusque and rude. Papa then replied in a low voice, and the woman again answered him rudely, as if he were no more than dirt. But my parents simply took it, standing before her as humbly as two peasants before a court official.

Then a large man in a suit came out of some back room somewhere and bellowed, "Mr. and Mrs. Calcines!"

My parents drew themselves up stiffly.

"Yes, sir," Papa said.

"You, Calcines, come with me. You, señora, you will go with her." The man indicated a different woman in an olive drab, government-issued skirt suit, with her hair in a bun and a cold, severe expression on her face. "You will be interrogated before leaving."

Mama and Papa looked at each other. They touched hands. Papa yanked at his shirt collar. Suddenly, his head twitched to the side, and he shrugged involuntarily. This was a twitch he'd developed over the last couple of years. It became worse every time he got upset or excited. I began to worry that they would think he was deranged. On the other hand, I thought maybe they would let us go sooner if they thought Papa had something contagious.

Mama and Papa followed the man and woman into separate rooms. Then the lady at the desk noticed me.

"What do you want?" she barked. "Do you have permission to be in here?"

"N-n-n-no, ma'am!"

"Outside!" said the lady.

I obeyed at once.

For the rest of the morning, Esther and I had to entertain each other on the sidewalk, under the watchful eye of the extremely patient taxi driver. Every time we asked him how much longer our parents would be, he gave the same philosophical shrug and said, "It will take as long as it takes, no more and no less."

Finally, after two hours, Mama and Papa came out the front door and down the steps. Both of them were pale and sweating. Papa had a piece of paper in his hand.

"Where have you been?" Esther shrieked. "We were getting scared!"

By the expressions on their faces, I knew the interrogations hadn't been pleasant. But by now I knew better than to ask what had happened. The only thing that mattered was that we were getting out.

"They're still letting us leave, right?" I asked.

Papa nodded. "I have our release form."

"Well, then, things are not so bad!" the driver said, his voice full of cheer.

Papa gave him directions to the place where we were to stay that night. It was a small room near the beach.

"Twenty-five pesos, please," said the driver when he dropped us off.

Twenty-five pesos was equal to about eight or nine American dollars. Mama reached into her purse for the money, which she had earned selling panetelas. I'd seen her count all of her money about thirty times on the way here, just to make sure she hadn't lost it. She handed the twenty-five pesos over. I had never seen so much cash before. I was impressed by how casually the driver tucked it into his shirt pocket. I wondered how we would have been able to afford the taxi if not for Mama's efforts, and all my trips to the port with those bags of panetelas.

The driver wished us well and asked that we please remember, if at all possible, to let his brother know he was okay. Then he was gone.

Tía Luisa and her daughter, Maricela, met us there, as we had arranged beforehand. They had come to Varadero to make sure that everything went well for us. It was only lunchtime. We had eaten nothing all day, and now, faced with the prospect of having the rest of the day and night to kill, I was hungry and restless.

"Let us kids go out and walk around," I said to Papa. "We'll be good, I promise."

Mama shook her head. "No!" she said. "It's too risky. All we need now is for you to get into trouble, hijo, and that is one thing you're very good at."

"Not today, Mama. I promise. I'll have Esther and Maricela along to keep me straight. Please, can we? What are we supposed to do, just sit in here all day and look at the floor?"

Finally they gave in. After ten minutes' worth of instructions and admonitions, we were set loose on Varadero Beach amid all the foreign tourists, in the place where no Cubans were supposed to go.

For at least half an hour, we did nothing but walk around and look at the stores. There were no soldiers or other security personnel in sight. I could hardly believe it. I couldn't even remember a time when armed people in uniform weren't standing around, watching our every move.

"This is what it will be like when we get to America, and even better," I told Esther. "Stores everywhere, all full of wonderful things, and no army men around to watch us."

"I'm nervous," said Maricela. "What if they *are* watching us?"

"Just act natural. Look, what's that shop?"

"It's an ice-cream parlor!" said Esther. "Oh, I wish we had money!"

As a matter of fact, I did have money—three pesos, which Abuela Ana had given me the night before. She'd earned them by selling eggs from her chickens, eggs that she and Abuelo were supposed to be eating for breakfast every morning. I also had the American dollar Papa had given me on my birthday, but I was certainly not going to spend that—at least, not until we got to America.

I showed the girls the money and told them where I'd gotten it. "Maybe it will be enough," I said.

"But Abuela went without breakfast all those mornings!" said Esther. "Would she really want us to spend it on ice cream?"

"Listen, hermana, we have to spend this money now, in Cuba," I told her, "because when we get to America these pesos won't be worth the paper they're printed on. All together they're not even worth one American dollar."

"Should we try?" Maricela asked.

"Well, why not?" I said. Being the man of the group, it was up to me to brave the possible wrath of the government by daring to purchase ice cream.

The girls waited for me outside. I went in, marveling that there was no line at the counter.

"Can I help you?" said the attendant, a man in a white uniform.

"Th—three chocolate ice creams, please," I said.

The man stared at me for a long moment. Then he shook his head. "No," he said.

Well, that was all I needed to hear. I turned and headed for the exit.

"Wait!" said the man. "What I meant was, you can't have three. You can only buy one per person. That's the rule."

I turned around again.

"In that case, sir," I said, "allow me to say that the other two are for the girls standing out there." I pointed to Esther and Maricela.

"Why don't they come in?"

"Too shy."

"Not from around here, huh?"

"No, sir. We're from Cienfuegos."

"We're only supposed to serve tourists here."

"If it makes any difference," I said, "we're leaving the country tomorrow. So I guess you could say we are tourists—kind of."

The man smiled.

"Your last ice cream in Cuba, eh? Well, then, I can certainly make an exception," he said, and he dug down with his scoop and made three chocolate ice-cream cones. I didn't tell him that this was also my first ice cream in Cuba. I was afraid he would laugh at me.

Outside on the sidewalk, I watched the girls as they licked their treats, smiling delightedly. Then I started on mine. So this was ice cream!

"Wow," I said when I'd finished it. "I knew it would be good, but I didn't think it would be *that* good!"

"I wish we could have shared it with Abuela, is all," said Esther. She started to sniffle. "Our poor grandparents, going without breakfast just so we can have ice cream! And it was gone so fast! Hermano, I wish we hadn't done it."

"Hermana, let it go," I said. "You're depressing me. Believe me, Abuela wouldn't mind. She knew it wasn't going to buy us much. She did it because she loves us."

"I remember I had ice cream once a long time ago," said Maricela. "But it didn't taste as good as this."

"Where we're going, we can have ice cream three times a day if we want to," I said. But Maricela looked so upset at this that I instantly regretted it.

"I'm sorry, Mari," I said. "I don't mean to rub it in."

"I know. It's exciting. I just wish I were going with you, that's all."

"Maybe someday you will come, too!" said Esther.

"Maybe," said Maricela, but she didn't sound too optimistic.

When we had licked the last smudge of chocolate from our fingers, we looked around for what to do next. Across the street, the ocean beckoned.

"I want to go down to the beach," I said.

"No!" said Esther. "Mama and Papa told us not to go too far!"

"It's right there!" I said. "Come on. When are we ever going to be here again? We're not going to do anything wrong. We're just going to look."

Finally, I convinced Esther it would be all right. The three of us crossed the street, took off our shoes, and went down to the water's edge. Varadero Beach was even more beautiful than the beach at Rancho Club, by Fort Jagua, which I had always thought was the most beautiful place in the world. As we stood with our feet in the warm surf, marveling at the shimmering beauty of the water and the glorious white sand, I remembered how the boys and I had sometimes bragged that we would bring our wives to Varadero on our honeymoons. In those days, I'd never seriously imagined I would be leaving Cuba. The telegram had seemed like a distant dream, not a serious possibility. Now here I was, about to leave. I wondered if my friends would ever even make it to this beach. Already, I had passed out of the sphere of everything that was familiar to us on San Carlos Street. My adventure had begun the moment we got into that taxi. I felt as if I were riding a rocket ship to the moon.

Soon, we went back to the room to find Mama and Papa relaxing on the two small single beds. Tía Luisa was about to go for a walk, no doubt to see if she could find any new black market contacts, and Maricela went with her. It was the first time I had seen my parents so relaxed in ages. Mama sat up.

"Where have you been?" she asked.

"Eduardito bought us ice cream!" said Esther.

"You kids are to stay close from now on," said Papa. He wasn't mad, just worried. Esther and I got into bed with him, and he pulled us close. For a moment, I flashed back to all those times we used to snuggle up with him when he came home for lunch from his job at Tío William's.

"Papa," I said, "tell us more about Ritica la Cubanita."

"Yeah, tell us about when you were little!" Esther said.

Papa sighed. "Those stories belong to a different time now," he said.

"What, you mean you won't tell them anymore?"

"No. I just mean that now we're living in moments that will be the stories of the future. I feel funny, like I just had a glimpse through time. You kids will be telling your own children about this moment when they are small, about the time you left Cuba and came to America. Your children will be Americans. And your grandchildren, too. This moment will be repeated in stories for generations, how the Calcineses had to flee their homeland forever."

"Eduardito is going to grow up and marry an American lady!" Esther giggled.

"Shut up!" I said. I was still young enough for such talk to embarrass me, at least in front of my parents. "You're going to marry an American man, too, Esther! He's going to have blond hair and blue eyes, and you're going to have to kiss him every day!"

"Oh, no!" said Esther. "I'm not kissing anybody!"

"Oh, yes, you are!"

"Children," Mama chided us. "Your father and I are tired. It's already been a very long day."

Papa was caressing my face absentmindedly, as he did sometimes. Suddenly he sat up and took my cheeks in his hands.

"Oh, no!" he declared, sounding horrified.

"What? What?" I panicked, thinking he'd remembered some reason why I couldn't go to America.

"Your face!"

"What about it? What? What?"

"Mama, look!" he said. "Look at your son! Specifically, look right under his nose!"

"I don't want to know," she said, in a tone that suggested she knew exactly what Papa was talking about.

"Papa, *what*?" I yelled.

"Come into the bathroom with me," Papa said.

He dragged me in front of the mirror and pushed my face close to it. He had me so worried I was nearly in tears. "I don't see anything!"

"You, my son," said Papa, "need a shave."

"What? A shave?"

"Yes. A shave. I see two, three, four, five . . . maybe ten whiskers there."

I began to laugh. "Papa, is that all? You scared me half to death!"

"Listen, niño. If the authorities think you're older than you really are, they might not let us go. So we're going to shave off that mustache right this minute, and tomorrow, when you get on the plane, act as young as possible."

"How do I do that?"

"I don't know. Suck your thumb or something."

"Papa! I'm not going to suck my thumb!"

"Well, I was just kidding. But we do need to trim you up. Go and get my razor from my luggage. I'm going to teach you how to use it. And when we get to America, I will get you a razor of your own."

I fetched his razor, and Papa lathered up a bit of soap and made a big show of covering my whole face with it. Then, instructing me carefully, he let me shave myself.

"It's a proud moment in a man's life when his son shaves for the first time," he said. "I remember very well the first time I shaved. My older brothers taught me, because my father was already gone. That seems like a million years ago."

"How old were you then, Papa?"

"I guess I must have been about the age you are now. We had already come to Cienfuegos." Papa sighed, remembering. "How hard it was, that trip. I'll never forget it. When we got to Cienfuegos, we felt we had arrived in the promised land. And now here we are, leaving it like it was a prison."

"It is a prison," Mama called from the next room. "Are you done yet? Let me see my clean-shaven boy. I want to see a smooth baby face, not a hairy man face."

I went to Mama's side. She touched my cheek, smiling.

"You really are almost a man," she said. "It's hard for a mama to see her little boy so grown up."

"What do you mean, hard?" I snorted. "My whole life you've been telling me to grow up, and now that I am, you don't like it!"

"It's complicated," Papa said. "When you have children, you'll understand how bittersweet it is to watch them grow older."

"Well, if you want, I can stay home and wear diapers for the rest of my life," I said. "Would that make you happy?"

Ordinarily, I might have gotten a tap on the bottom for such mouthiness. But under the circumstances, we all needed a good laugh. Mama and Papa and Esther were convulsed with mirth for the next few minutes. Even I had a good chuckle over my little joke.

No one slept that night. We tossed and turned until finally a glimmer of pink began to show on the horizon. Papa got up and threw open the curtains.

"Well, it's morning!" he announced. "Time to get ready!"

I was so dazed with exhaustion and excitement that I remember little of what followed. I presume we got washed and dressed, packed up our few belongings, said goodbye to Tía Luisa and Maricela, and then waited outside for the taxi to take us to the airport. Of the ride itself, I remember nothing, except that all of us were so keyed up we couldn't sit still, not even Mama.

The next clear memory I have is of standing on a runway, next to a giant Pan Am plane. Esther and I stared up at it, awestruck. The only airplanes we'd ever seen had been miles over our heads. Now we were about to go inside one.

There was, of course, a uniformed military officer standing guard at the portable stairway. This one was a woman. When she saw us coming, she held up her hand for us to stop.

"Calcines family?"

"Yes," said Papa, as he handed her the government release form.

"There's a problem," she said.

We all tried not to groan.

"What's the problem, ma'am?" Mama asked.

"You haven't been assigned seats yet. There may not be room for you on this airplane."

"What?" Papa said, desperation in his voice. "Ma'am, how can this be? They must have known we were coming. If we miss this flight, will they let us board another one?"

The woman shrugged. "How should I know?" she said. "It's not my problem. You want to leave the country like a bunch of worms, you have to take what you're given. Maybe you think you deserve first-class seats, too. Is that what you think?"

Aha, I thought. So this was the problem—they were going to take one last dig at us before sending us on our way.

Papa began to lose his cool. His twitch, under control all morning, came back with a vengeance. He paced back and forth on the runway, just feet away from the stairs. Mama, Esther, and I stared up at the doorway of the plane, where a beautiful stewardess stood, smiling as the other passengers embarked.

Esther elbowed me.

"Look at that lady!" she said. "She has blond hair!"

"She sure does," I said. It wasn't the first time we had seen a blond person, but something about the sight of this woman seemed auspicious. Soon we would be in the land of blond people. The fact that she was there was comforting, as if she were an angelic ambassador sent to make us feel welcome.

After a while, and for no discernible reason, the woman officer who was holding us back said, "Well, I guess you can board now."

"Well, thank you very much," said Papa, obviously trying to keep the sarcasm from his voice.

We mounted the stairs and climbed into the plane. The stewardess said something to us in English. We smiled politely and followed as she led us to our seats. These were more luxurious and comfortable than any piece of furniture we had ever owned. I was captivated by the fact that I could raise and lower the back, and I spent several minutes experimenting with the best position. Finally, the gentleman behind me cleared his throat, and Papa told me to cut it out. Then Esther discovered a little drop-down table in front of her and undid the latch. The table flopped open with a clatter.

"Don't!" I said, pushing it back up. "You want to get us kicked off the plane? You're going to ruin everything!"

"I'm sorry," Esther whispered.

Just then a stewardess came by with a trolley.

"Coke while we wait for takeoff?" she inquired sweetly.

I looked at Papa, who looked at Mama, who looked confused.

"What did she say?" Papa asked.

"She wants to give us something," I said. "Coca-Cola, I think."

"Tell her we can't afford it," said Mama.

"How am I supposed to tell her that?" Papa said. "What am I, a professor of English all of a sudden? Hijo, you tell her."

"Me! I can barely speak proper Spanish!" I exclaimed. "How am I going to tell her?"

This debate might have gone on for another hour if the woman hadn't figured out what was happening. In a few deft moves, she had unlatched all our tables, opened four cans of Coke, and set them before us—along with plastic cups of ice and bags of peanuts. We were as stunned as if she had just turned into Santa Claus and filled our laps with presents.

"It's free!" Papa said.

"Free? How can they give it away for free?" Mama wondered.

"Who cares!" I said. I poured myself a drink of Coke on ice and took a long, slow sip. It was the most delicious beverage I'd ever tasted in my life. Then I opened my bag of peanuts and crunched each of them one by one, making them last as long as possible. *If only the boys could see me now!*

The stewardess began to collect cups and an intercom crackled to life, and a voice began to ramble in English. As I listened, I realized with a sinking heart that somehow I was going to have to master this language, and that it was going to be very hard.

"It sounds like plates breaking," complained Esther. "How can people make those noises?"

"We'll have to learn this kind of talk," I told her.

"Well, how are we going to do that? I can't understand a word!"

"I guess from practicing."

"Great."

Then the captain switched to Spanish, a language with which he was clearly not comfortable.

"Hello, traveling peoples!" he said. "You are going now in an airplane. We are going to take a short flight. We are going to Miami of Florida of America!"

We looked at one another, amused.

"The time of our flying will be forty-five little minutes," continued the captain. "If you are wanting something, just ask the pretty ladies! They help you good. Have nice days!"

"That was the worst Spanish I've ever heard," Papa said in wonderment.

"He gets an A for effort," Mama said.

"His Spanish is better than our English," I reminded them.

Then the plane began to move. I looked out the window as the landscape rolled past, slowly first, then faster and faster.

"Papa, look how fast we're going!" I said.

"Shh, niño! I need to concentrate!" Papa said.

I looked at him. His eyes were shut, and he was gripping the arms of his chair as though trying to fly the plane through sheer force of will.

"Felo! Relax!" said Mama. "You're going to have a heart attack!"

"Let the pilot fly the plane, Papa," I said. "Your job is just to sit here."

At that moment, the nose of the plane lifted, and the ground began to fall away beneath us. Papa began praying out loud to Santa Barbara. Mama put her hands to her mouth and watched in disbelief out the window as we rose toward the clouds. Esther and I giggled and nudged each other as we looked down at the ground, now far, far below us. The ocean came into view, breathtaking and dazzling in its glory. Then, suddenly, we were surrounded by mist.

A few minutes later we came out on top of the clouds. At this, I was full of astonishment. I knew airplanes went high, but not *that* high. I stared out at the fluffy white floor. It looked solid enough to walk on.

I had barely had time enough to look at everything when the captain came on the intercom again and prattled in English for a while. Then he switched to Spanish.

"Ladies and gentlemen," he said casually, "we have just come inside the airspace of America. Welcome to the United States."

It took a few moments for his words to sink in, and then we hugged and cried.

We were free!

Epilogue

As for me today, I am only a man who is striving to live each day in a state of humility. I live in Tampa, where I own a couple of small businesses. I ran for the office of state representative in 2000, and although I was not elected, I felt a great sense of joy and success in having attempted to give back to a land that I love, the land that had adopted me and granted me freedom. Just being able to run in the election meant a lot to me, because obviously such a thing would never have been possible in Cuba.

Like all baseball fans, I never lost my love of the game. I am now the owner of the Gallo Sports Agency, representing professional ballplayers and providing scholarship opportunities to lots of kids who otherwise would never have the chance to play. I also own a hair studio, work with at-risk students in my community and in the public school system, and am hard at work on upcoming books. And my newest project is the formation of the Tampa West Community Development Corporation, which will focus on developing programs to help youth and less fortunate families.

My life is filled with other gifts, too. On December 9, 2008, Mercy and I celebrated our thirtieth wedding anniversary. We became American citizens in 1991—one of the proudest days of our lives. Our sons are both attending universities, to our immense pride. Papa unfortunately passed away on April 7, 1978, at the age of forty-nine. Although too young to die, he lived nine glorious years as a free, family-loving man in what he considered the great United States. Mama is still a tough cookie and has survived the many heartaches life has brought her. She retired a few years ago after working in textile factories for thirty years. She lives with my sister, Esther, who is the mother of two wonderful children and has worked for many years as a customer service agent in the corporate world. Her oldest daughter became a university graduate in May 2008, and her son is a bright twelve-year-old middle schooler. My cousin and childhood pal, Luis, came to Florida soon after I did. He and his wife have been married for over twenty years, and are blessed with two wonderful sons.

Every morning when I wake up, I give thanks because I live in the "Land of Freedom to the north," as we used to call America. I can hear Abuelo's voice in my ear as if he were standing right next to me, and feel his work-worn hand on my shoulder. *Remember that every day is a gift. Each morning, you should greet the sun as though it were your bride. Take pride in your appearance, and behave respectfully to everyone.* The older I get, the more wisdom I find in the words of this simple, God-fearing man.

I yearn to someday go back to Glorytown when Cuba is free. Tío William, the giant of my youth, is no longer with us. I feel a strong need to sit beside his grave and tell him some of my stories about life in America. I want to bask once more in the presence of the man who vowed not to let the Communists get the better of him, to remind him about the time when, with all the suffering he had undergone, he still managed to find it in himself to toss me diez centavos, and to be my hero.

Once more, I will walk down San Carlos Street, past the Jagua Movie House; past the front door of number 6110, where my dear grandparents lived; and past our little house across the street. I even want to see the shambling old wreck that La Natividad lived in—and I will not be surprised in the slightest if I see La Natividad herself coming down the steps with her umbrella, ageless thanks to her black magic. And I want to see my old childhood buddy Tito, to tell him how often I still think of him and Rolando, who was killed by lightning shortly after we left Cuba, and those endless days in Glorytown.

Most of all, even though I am an American now, I want to return just once more to the place I often revisit in my dreams, to feel the soft warmth of the Caribbean evenings, to see the turquoise waters and the white sand . . . to the place that I once knew.

My beloved Glorytown!

Acknowledgments

Above all, I give all glory and honor to almighty God. I would also like to give praise to my wife, Mercy, and our sons, Christian and Gabriel. Your love is the essence of my existence. To you, Mama, for your love, guidance, and courage. Sister Esther and her children, Rebeca and Luis, you are dearly loved. Thanks to my devoted agent, Doris Booth, for believing in me. Gracias, Ramón. To my editor, partner, and friend, the author William Kowalski, you brought life and literary quality to my story. To Luis, Tito, and Rolando for the childhood memories, in those endless days under the sun. Special thanks to my clients and friends who through the years encouraged me to pursue the writing of my story. You are deeply woven into the fiber of who I am. To Sandy Berquist and the author Max Courson, and to the memory of Carolyn Benish—this work might never have happened if it wasn't for your enthusiastic support. To Ken Silbert, Bill Boroughs, and Bill Reynolds for your friendship. To Janie Faust and Pat Sexton for your spiritual guidance and support. Lastly, I give honor and praise to the dissidents fighting for human rights in Cuba, who continue to be persecuted but remain peacefully loyal to their cause of freedom. May the world hear your pleading voice through this book.